# BALI UNVEILED: A PREPARATION GUIDE

**TOMAS GRAY**

All rights reserved. No part of this publication may be reproduced, distributed, or transmitted in any form or by any means, including photocopying, recording, or other electronic or mechanical methods, without the prior written permission of the publisher, except in the case of brief quotations embodied in critical reviews and certain other noncommercial uses permitted by copyright law.

Copyright © (TOMAS GRAY) (2023).

# TABLE OF CONTENTS

**CHAPTER 1: Introduction** — 7
   1.1 Welcome to Bali: The Island of Gods — 7
**CHAPTER 2: Essential Travel Information** — 11
   2.1 Travel Planning Tips — 11
   2.2 Visa and Entry Requirements — 16
   2.3 Currency and Money Matters — 20
   2.4 Health and Safety Tips — 24
   2.5 Packing Essentials — 29
**CHAPTER 3: Getting to Know Bali** — 35
   3.1 Geography and Regions — 35
      Overview of Bali's Geography: — 35
   3.2 Climate and Best Time to Visit — 39
   3.3 Cultural Etiquette and Customs — 42
**CHAPTER 4: Top Destinations** — 47
   4.1 Exploring Ubud: Cultural Heart of Bali — 47
   4.2 Relaxing in Seminyak and Canggu — 50
   4.3 Stunning Beaches of Kuta and Legian — 54
   4.4 Tranquility in Uluwatu and Bukit Peninsula — 57
   4.5 Lovina: North Bali's Hidden Gem — 60
   4.6 East Bali Adventures: Candidasa and Amed — 64
**CHAPTER 5: Activities for Everyone** — 69
   5.1 Family-Friendly Attractions — 69
   5.1.1 Waterbom Bali — 72
   5.1.2 Bali Safari and Marine Park — 76
   5.1.3 Bali Treetop Adventure Park — 79
   5.2 Romantic Experiences for Couples — 82
   5.2.1 Sunset at Tanah Lot Temple — 87

| | |
|---|---|
| 5.2.2 Romantic Beach Dinners | 90 |
| 5.2.3 Spa and Wellness Retreats | 94 |
| **CHAPTER 6: Exploring Nature and Adventure** | **99** |
| 6.1 Mount Batur Sunrise Trek | 99 |
| 6.2 Sacred Monkey Forest Sanctuary | 102 |
| 6.3 Scenic Rice Terraces of Tegalalang | 105 |
| 6.4 Diving and Snorkeling in Menjangan | 109 |
| 6.5 Water Sports in Nusa Dua | 112 |
| **CHAPTER 7: Cultural Immersion** | **117** |
| 7.1 Temples and Sacred Sites | 117 |
| 7.1.1 Besakih Temple | 120 |
| 7.1.2 Uluwatu Temple | 123 |
| 7.1.3 Tirta Empul Temple | 127 |
| 7.2 Traditional Balinese Dance Performances | 130 |
| 7.3 Art Markets and Handicrafts | 134 |
| 7.4 Balinese Cooking Classes | 137 |
| **CHAPTER 8: Indulging in Balinese Cuisine** | **141** |
| 8.1 Must-Try Dishes and Local Delicacies | 141 |
| 8.2 Popular Warungs and Restaurants | 145 |
| 8.3 Vegan and Vegetarian Options | 148 |
| **CHAPTER 9: Practical Tips for a Smooth Trip** | **153** |
| 9.1 Accommodation Options | 153 |
| 9.2 Getting Around: Transportation Guide | 157 |
| Modes of Transportation | 157 |
| Navigating Bali's Roads | 159 |
| Safety Considerations | 160 |
| Getting to and From the Airport | 161 |
| Exploring Beyond the Tourist Hubs | 161 |

| | |
|---|---|
| Environmental Considerations | 162 |
| 9.3 Language Basics | 163 |
| Bahasa Indonesia: The National Language | 163 |
| Local Dialects and Languages | 164 |
| English: A Bridge to Communication | 164 |
| Non-Verbal Communication | 165 |
| Cultural Sensitivity and Language | 166 |
| Language Learning Resources | 166 |
| 9.4 Internet and Communication | 167 |
| Internet Connectivity in Bali | 167 |
| Mobile Networks and Coverage | 168 |
| Communication Apps | 169 |
| Cafes and Co-Working Spaces | 170 |
| Cultural Considerations | 170 |
| **CHAPTER 10: Itineraries for Every Traveler** | **173** |
| 10.1 3 Days in Bali: Family-Focused Itinerary | 173 |
| 10.2 5 Days in Bali: Romantic Escape | 177 |
| 10.3 7 Days in Bali: Adventure and Culture | 178 |
| **CHAPTER 11: Additional Resources** | **181** |
| 11.1 Useful Apps and Websites | 181 |
| 11.2 Emergency Contacts | 184 |

# CHAPTER 1: Introduction

## 1.1 Welcome to Bali: The Island of Gods

Nestled in the heart of Indonesia, Bali stands as a beguiling jewel of the archipelago, captivating travelers with its mystical allure, diverse landscapes, and rich cultural tapestry. Often referred to as the "Island of Gods," Bali offers an enchanting blend of ancient traditions, pristine beaches, lush rice terraces, and vibrant artistic expressions. From the moment you set foot on this remarkable island, you'll be swept away by its palpable spirituality, warm hospitality, and breathtaking beauty.

### A Glimpse into Bali's Mystique

Bali's nickname, "Island of Gods," is no mere moniker; it encapsulates the island's deep-rooted spiritual identity. Balinese Hinduism, a unique blend of indigenous beliefs and Indian influences, permeates every facet of daily life. Intricately carved temples, known as "Pura," grace every corner, with offerings of flowers and incense filling the air, honoring gods and ancestors. The Balinese people's unwavering devotion is not just a ritual, but a way of life that envelops visitors in an aura of reverence.

## Nature's Kaleidoscope

As you traverse the island, you'll find that Bali's landscapes are as diverse as its spiritual practices. The verdant rice terraces of Tegalalang present a symphony of emerald hues, a testament to the Balinese people's deep connection with the land and their devotion to the cultivation of rice. Mount Batur, an active volcano, offers the opportunity for a thrilling sunrise trek, rewarding adventurers with panoramic vistas that seem to stretch to infinity. The azure waters of the Indian Ocean kiss Bali's shores, creating paradisiacal beaches that cater to both relaxation and adventure.

## Cultural Richness and Artistic Flourish

The pulse of Bali's artistic heart beats strong, evident in its captivating dance performances, intricate wood carvings, and vibrant paintings. The traditional Kecak dance, with its haunting chants and hypnotic choreography, transports audiences to another realm. Ubud, the cultural epicenter of the island, entices art enthusiasts with its galleries and workshops, where you can witness master artisans at work, shaping wood, stone, and canvas into expressions of profound beauty.

## A Tapestry of Festivals and Rituals

Bali's calendar is adorned with an array of festivals and ceremonies, infusing everyday life with a sense of wonder. The Galungan festival, a celebration of the triumph of good over evil, sees every village adorned with colorful penjor (decorative bamboo poles) and offerings. Nyepi, the Day of Silence, is a truly unique experience, as the entire island shuts down in meditation and reflection, offering a rare opportunity for introspection amidst the cacophony of modern life.

## The Warm Embrace of Balinese Hospitality

Bali's greatest treasure lies in the genuine warmth and hospitality of its people. A simple "Selamat Datang" (Welcome) is more than just a greeting; it's an invitation to embrace the island's embrace and immerse yourself in its culture. The Balinese people are known for their genuine smiles, open hearts, and a willingness to share their traditions with visitors. Whether you're partaking in a traditional ceremony, joining a local family for a meal, or engaging in conversation with a street vendor, you'll feel an overwhelming sense of connection and belonging.

## Embarking on Your Bali Journey

As you embark on your journey through Bali, remember that this mystical island is not merely a destination; it's an experience that touches the soul and leaves an indelible mark. Whether you're seeking spiritual enlightenment, cultural enrichment, or simply a moment of respite in nature's embrace, Bali welcomes you with open arms. Allow yourself to be enchanted by the island's beauty, humbled by its spirituality, and enriched by its traditions. Let Bali, the Island of Gods, work its magic on you, and in return, you'll carry a piece of its mystique with you, long after your departure.

## CHAPTER 2: Essential Travel Information

### *2.1 Travel Planning Tips*

Traveling can be an exhilarating and transformative experience, offering the chance to explore new destinations, immerse oneself in different cultures, and create lasting memories. However, a successful trip doesn't happen by chance; it requires thoughtful planning and preparation. Whether you're an experienced globetrotter or a first-time traveler, these travel planning tips will help ensure a smooth and enjoyable journey.

**1. Set Clear Objectives:**
Before you begin planning, define the purpose of your trip. Are you seeking relaxation, adventure, cultural exploration, or something else? Having a clear objective will guide your decisions regarding destination, activities, and accommodations.

**2. Choose the Right Destination:**
Research potential destinations based on your interests, budget, and travel style. Consider factors such as climate, language, safety, and local customs. Make a list of places that align with your objectives.

**3. Create a Budget:**

Establish a realistic budget that encompasses all aspects of your trip, including transportation, accommodation, meals, activities, and souvenirs. Be sure to account for unexpected expenses as well.

### 4. Research Thoroughly:
Delve into detailed research about your chosen destination. Learn about local customs, traditions, and etiquette. Familiarize yourself with the top attractions, local cuisine, and transportation options.

### 5. Decide on Travel Duration:
Determine the ideal length of your trip. Consider the time needed to fully experience your chosen destination without feeling rushed.

### 6. Travel Dates and Seasons:
Research the best time to visit your destination in terms of weather, crowds, and events. Prices for accommodations and flights can vary greatly depending on the season.

### 7. Book Flights and Accommodation Early:
Once you've decided on travel dates, book your flights and accommodations as early as possible to secure the best deals and availability.

**8. Travel Documents and Vaccinations:**

Ensure you have a valid passport and any necessary visas well in advance. Research if any vaccinations are required or recommended for your destination.

**9. Pack Light and Smart:**

Create a packing list based on the climate and activities at your destination. Pack versatile clothing and essential items, and remember to leave room for souvenirs. Don't forget chargers, adapters, and any necessary medications.

**10. Travel Insurance:**

Invest in comprehensive travel insurance to cover unexpected events such as trip cancellations, medical emergencies, or lost luggage.

**11. Plan Activities and Sightseeing:**

Create a rough itinerary of the activities and attractions you want to experience each day. However, be flexible to allow for spontaneous discoveries and relaxation.

**12. Local Transportation:**

Research local transportation options, such as public transit, taxis, or ride-sharing services.

Familiarize yourself with routes, schedules, and costs.

### 13. Learn Basic Local Phrases:
Learning a few phrases in the local language can go a long way in enhancing your travel experience and connecting with locals.

### 14. Stay Connected:
Arrange for international roaming or purchase a local SIM card to stay connected with family and friends. Additionally, download offline maps and translation apps to navigate unfamiliar areas.

### 15. Stay Healthy and Safe:
Prioritize your health and safety by staying hydrated, using sunscreen, and practicing good hygiene. Research local customs and safety tips to avoid any potential risks.

### 16. Respect Local Culture:
Embrace the local culture with an open mind and a respectful attitude. Dress appropriately, observe local customs, and be mindful of cultural norms.

### 17. Backup Important Documents:

Make digital copies of important documents such as your passport, visas, and travel insurance. Store them securely online in case of loss or theft.

**18. Notify Your Bank:**
Inform your bank about your travel plans to avoid any issues with using your credit or debit cards abroad.

**19. Stay Flexible:**
Despite careful planning, things may not always go as planned. Embrace the unexpected and stay flexible in your approach to ensure a positive experience.

**20. Capture Memories:**
Bring a camera or smartphone to capture the highlights of your journey. Take photos and journal your experiences to cherish the memories for years to come.

Successful travel planning involves a combination of research, organization, and flexibility. By following these travel planning tips, you can maximize your travel experience, create unforgettable memories, and navigate new destinations with confidence. Remember, the journey itself is just as important as the destination. Happy travels!

## 2.2 *Visa and Entry Requirements*

Planning a trip to Bali, Indonesia, promises an incredible experience filled with lush landscapes, vibrant culture, and breathtaking beaches. To ensure a seamless journey, it's crucial to understand the visa and entry requirements for your destination. This comprehensive guide will provide you with all the information you need to navigate the visa process and enjoy a worry-free vacation in Bali.

**Visa Exemptions and Visa on Arrival:**
For many nationalities, Bali offers convenient visa exemptions and a Visa on Arrival (VOA) option. These allow eligible travelers to enter Indonesia without obtaining a visa in advance. Here's what you need to know:

1. Visa Exemption: Citizens of certain countries are eligible for a visa exemption, which allows them to stay in Indonesia for up to 30 days for tourism purposes. This period cannot be extended. It's important to note that the visa exemption cannot be converted into another type of visa.

2. Visa on Arrival (VOA): If your nationality is not eligible for a visa exemption, you can obtain a Visa on Arrival upon arrival at Bali's international airports. The VOA is valid for a stay of up to 30 days and can be extended once for an additional 30 days.

**Visa Extensions:**
If you wish to stay in Bali for more than 30 days (including the initial 30 days from the visa exemption or VOA), you'll need to apply for a visa extension. The extension can be done at the local immigration office and typically requires completing paperwork, paying a fee, and undergoing a biometric process. It's recommended to initiate the extension process well before your initial 30-day period expires to avoid overstaying your visa and potential fines.

**Tourist Visas:**
For travelers planning an extended stay beyond the 60-day limit of the visa exemption and VOA, applying for a tourist visa before arriving in Indonesia is recommended. The tourist visa is valid for 60 days and can be extended for another 30 days at the local immigration office.

**Required Documents:**

Whether you're arriving with a visa exemption, VOA, or a tourist visa, you'll need the following documents:

- A passport with at least six months of validity from your entry date.

- Proof of return or onward travel (flight ticket or itinerary).

- Sufficient funds to cover your stay.

- Completed visa application forms (if applicable).

- Passport-sized photos meeting specific criteria.

- Appropriate visa fees in cash (for VOA and extensions).

- Any additional documents required by the immigration authorities.

**Overstaying Penalties:**
Overstaying your visa in Indonesia comes with penalties, which can range from daily fines to deportation. To avoid this, ensure that you leave the country before your visa or visa extension expires.

**Visa Information Resources:**
To stay up to date with visa regulations and requirements, consult the official website of the Indonesian Embassy or Consulate in your home country. They provide accurate and current information regarding visa policies.

**Entry and Customs Requirements:**
Apart from visa-related documents, you should also be aware of the following entry and customs requirements:

- Health-related documentation, including vaccination certificates (if required).

- Custom declaration forms for items you're bringing into the country.

- Respect local laws and customs, as Bali is a region with deep cultural and religious traditions.

**Travel Insurance:**
Travel insurance is essential for any international trip, including your journey to Bali. Ensure your policy covers medical emergencies, trip cancellations, lost luggage, and other unforeseen events.

**Plan Ahead:**
To avoid any last-minute complications, it's advisable to plan your visa and entry requirements well in advance. Double-check all documents and requirements before departing for Bali.

Understanding the visa and entry requirements for a trip to Bali is a fundamental aspect of ensuring a smooth and enjoyable travel experience. By familiarizing yourself with the available visa options, requirements, and necessary documentation, you'll be well-prepared to explore Bali's stunning landscapes, immerse yourself in its vibrant culture, and create unforgettable memories during your stay.

## *2.3 Currency and Money Matters*

Bali, Indonesia, is a popular travel destination known for its stunning landscapes, vibrant culture, and warm hospitality. As you plan your trip to this enchanting island, it's essential to familiarize yourself with the local currency, banking facilities, currency exchange options, and money-related tips to ensure a smooth and enjoyable experience. In this guide, we'll provide an extensive overview of currency and money matters in Bali.

**Currency: Indonesian Rupiah (IDR)**

The official currency of Bali and Indonesia is the Indonesian Rupiah (IDR). It's denoted by the symbol "Rp" and is often referred to as "rupiah." The currency is available in both coins and banknotes, with various denominations catering to different spending levels. While some places may accept major foreign currencies (such as US Dollars or Euros), it's best to use Indonesian Rupiah for your transactions to avoid unfavorable exchange rates.

**Currency Denominations:**
Indonesian Rupiah banknotes come in denominations of 1,000, 2,000, 5,000, 10,000, 20,000, 50,000, and 100,000. Coins are also available in smaller denominations such as 100, 200, 500, and 1,000 rupiah.

**Currency Exchange:**
Currency exchange services are widely available in Bali, especially in tourist areas, airports, and major cities. You can exchange foreign currency or traveler's checks at banks, currency exchange offices, and hotels. It's advisable to compare exchange rates and fees to get the best value for your money. Be cautious of unlicensed money changers, as they may offer better rates but could be involved in fraudulent practices.

**ATMs and Banking:**
ATMs are prevalent throughout Bali and are a convenient way to access cash. Look for ATMs affiliated with well-known banks to ensure secure transactions. Major credit and debit cards are widely accepted in hotels, restaurants, and upscale establishments. However, it's a good idea to carry some cash for smaller purchases and places that don't accept cards.

**Currency Conversion Tips:**
1. Be Mindful of Exchange Rates: Exchange rates can vary between different providers. Research current rates online before exchanging money to ensure you get a fair deal.

2. Withdraw Larger Amounts: ATM withdrawal fees can add up, so consider withdrawing larger amounts of money to reduce the number of transactions and associated fees.

3. Inform Your Bank: Let your bank know about your travel plans to avoid potential issues with using your cards abroad. Verify whether your cards have international transaction fees.

4. Carry Smaller Denominations: Smaller denominations can be useful for small purchases, tips, and markets where exact change is appreciated.

**Tipping Etiquette:**
Tipping is not obligatory in Bali, but it's a common practice in the service industry. In restaurants, adding a 5-10% service charge to the bill is typical. If a service charge isn't included, leaving a small tip for excellent service is appreciated. For drivers, tour guides, and hotel staff, tipping is a gesture of gratitude for their assistance.

**Haggling and Bargaining:**
Haggling is common in Bali's markets and shops, especially in areas like Ubud and Seminyak. While it's expected, remember to do so respectfully. Start with a lower offer and work your way up until a mutually agreed-upon price is reached.

**Budgeting:**
Bali offers a range of accommodation, dining, and entertainment options catering to various budgets. Luxury resorts, boutique hotels, local eateries, and street food stalls provide diverse choices. Research and create a budget that suits your preferences and travel style.

**Travel Insurance:**
Invest in comprehensive travel insurance that covers medical emergencies, trip cancellations, lost luggage, and other unforeseen events. This ensures financial protection during your trip.

Being well-prepared regarding currency and money matters is essential for a hassle-free experience in Bali. Understanding the local currency, exchanging money wisely, and following appropriate tipping etiquette will enhance your interactions and help you make the most of your time on this captivating island. With the right approach to managing your finances, you'll be able to fully immerse yourself in Bali's rich culture, natural beauty, and vibrant atmosphere.

### *2.4 Health and Safety Tips*

Bali, with its idyllic beaches, lush landscapes, and rich culture, is a dream destination for travelers. To make the most of your journey and ensure your well-being, it's essential to prioritize health and safety. From understanding local health risks to knowing how to stay safe while exploring, this comprehensive guide will equip you with the knowledge you need for a worry-free and enjoyable trip to Bali.

**Health Precautions:**

1. Vaccinations: Before traveling to Bali, consult a travel health clinic or your healthcare provider to ensure you're up to date with routine vaccinations. Additionally, consider vaccinations for diseases such as hepatitis A, typhoid, and tetanus.

2. Food and Water Safety: While Bali offers a variety of delicious cuisine, be cautious about consuming street food and tap water. Stick to bottled or boiled water, and choose food vendors with high levels of cleanliness and popularity.

3. Mosquito Protection: Bali is in a region where mosquito-borne diseases such as dengue fever and Zika virus are a concern. Use insect repellent, wear long sleeves and pants, and sleep under mosquito nets if necessary.

4. Sun Protection: The tropical climate in Bali means strong sun exposure. Apply sunscreen with a high SPF, wear sunglasses, a hat, and lightweight clothing to protect yourself from UV rays.

**Medical Facilities:**

1. Healthcare Facilities: Bali has reputable medical facilities and hospitals, especially in tourist areas. Familiarize yourself with the locations of medical centers and clinics nearest to your accommodation.

2. Travel Insurance: Comprehensive travel insurance is a must. Ensure your policy covers medical emergencies, hospitalization, medical evacuations, and repatriation.

**Local Customs and Etiquette:**

1. Dress Modestly: Bali is a culturally rich destination with deep Hindu traditions. Dress modestly, especially when visiting temples or rural areas. Cover your shoulders and knees as a sign of respect.

2. Respectful Behavior: Balinese people are warm and welcoming. Show respect by using appropriate greetings, removing your shoes before entering homes or temples, and participating in local customs with humility.

**Safety Tips:**

1. Traffic and Transportation: Traffic in Bali can be chaotic. Use reputable transportation options, wear

helmets if renting a motorbike, and exercise caution when crossing roads.

2. Swimming Safety: Bali's beaches are alluring, but be cautious of strong currents and riptides. Swim in designated areas and follow lifeguard instructions. Consider local advice on safe swimming conditions.

3. Scams and Petty Crime: Like any tourist destination, be cautious of scams and petty theft. Keep your belongings secure, avoid displaying valuables, and use hotel safes for important documents.

4. Natural Hazards: Bali is in a region with potential for natural disasters such as earthquakes and volcanic activity. Stay informed about your surroundings and follow local authorities' instructions if any warnings are issued.

**Emergency Contacts:**

Make a note of important contact numbers:

- Medical emergencies: 118 or 119

- Police: 110

- Tourist Police: (0361) 754 599

**Travel Advisory:**

Stay informed about travel advisories and safety updates from your country's embassy or consulate. They provide valuable information about local conditions and safety concerns.

**Cultural Sensitivity:**

Immerse yourself in Bali's vibrant culture while being respectful. Seek permission before taking photos of locals, ask questions about customs, and engage in cultural activities with a genuine interest.

**Environmental Responsibility:**

Respect Bali's natural beauty by avoiding littering, supporting eco-friendly practices, and participating in organized beach cleanups if available.

A successful and enjoyable trip to Bali hinges on your commitment to health and safety. By prioritizing vaccinations, adhering to local customs, and following safety guidelines, you'll create lasting memories while safeguarding your well-being. Embrace Bali's cultural richness, natural beauty, and warm hospitality, and embark on your journey with confidence and preparedness.

## *2.5 Packing Essentials*

Preparing for a trip to Bali, Indonesia, requires thoughtful consideration of your packing list. The island's tropical climate, diverse activities, and unique culture demand a well-curated collection of essentials. Whether you're lounging on the beach, exploring cultural sites, or enjoying outdoor adventures, this comprehensive guide will help you pack wisely and ensure you have everything you need for a memorable and comfortable journey.

## Clothing:

1. Lightweight Clothing: Pack lightweight, breathable clothing to combat Bali's warm climate. Include tank tops, t-shirts, shorts, and dresses. Opt for moisture-wicking fabrics that dry quickly.

2. Swimwear: Bali's beautiful beaches and resorts call for swimwear. Don't forget cover-ups, rash guards, and board shorts for added sun protection.

3. Modest Attire: When visiting temples or rural areas, dress modestly with long-sleeve tops, pants,

or a sarong. Pack a shawl or scarf to cover your shoulders when necessary.

4. Comfortable Footwear: Pack comfortable walking shoes, sandals, and flip-flops. Closed-toe shoes are essential for outdoor activities and exploring.

5. Rain Gear: Bali experiences a wet season. Bring a lightweight, waterproof jacket and a foldable umbrella.

**Accessories:**

1. Sun Protection: Don't forget sunglasses with UV protection, a wide-brimmed hat, and a high SPF sunscreen.

2. Swim Accessories: Pack a beach towel, waterproof phone pouch, and a dry bag to keep your belongings safe at the beach.

3. Electronics: Bring your smartphone, camera, and chargers. A power bank can be a lifesaver for keeping devices charged during your adventures.

4. Adapters: Indonesia uses Type C and F sockets. Bring the appropriate adapter to charge your devices.

## Health and Toiletries:

1. Medications: Carry prescription medications in their original containers, along with a copy of the prescription. Basic first aid supplies, such as bandages and pain relievers, are useful.

2. Insect Repellent: Bali's tropical environment means mosquitos are prevalent. Pack mosquito repellent with DEET or natural alternatives.

3. Personal Hygiene Items: Essentials like toothbrush, toothpaste, soap, shampoo, and conditioner. Consider biodegradable options to minimize your environmental impact.

## Documentation:

1. Passport: Ensure your passport is valid for at least six months beyond your travel dates.

2. Visa Documents: Carry necessary visa-related documents, including printed copies of your visa approval or VOA.

3. Travel Insurance: Keep a printed copy of your travel insurance policy and emergency contact information.

**Miscellaneous:**

1. Cash and Cards: Bring a mix of local currency (Indonesian Rupiah) and a credit/debit card. Notify your bank about your travel plans.

2. Reusable Water Bottle: Help reduce plastic waste by carrying a reusable water bottle to refill throughout your trip.

3. Daypack: A small backpack is perfect for day trips, carrying essentials, and storing your belongings securely.

4. Language Guide: While many Balinese locals speak English, carrying a basic Indonesian language guide can enhance your interactions.

**Cultural Considerations:**

1. Sarong or Wrap: A versatile sarong can be used as a beach cover-up, temple attire, or even a lightweight blanket.

2. Offering Items: If you plan to visit temples, pack a small offering kit, which usually includes flowers and incense.

3. Gifts: Small souvenirs from your home country can be appreciated as gifts for Balinese hosts or new friends you make.

Environmental Awareness:

1. Reusable Bag: Carry a foldable reusable bag for shopping, reducing plastic waste.

2. Eco-Friendly Toiletries: Use biodegradable or eco-friendly toiletries to minimize your environmental footprint.

Packing for Bali requires a balance of practicality and cultural sensitivity. By including essential clothing, accessories, health items, and documentation, you'll be well-prepared to embrace Bali's beauty, engage in diverse activities, and respect its rich cultural traditions. Prioritize comfort, sun protection, and sustainability, and you'll be ready for an unforgettable journey on this enchanting island.

## CHAPTER 3: Getting to Know Bali

### *3.1 Geography and Regions*

Bali, often referred to as the "Island of the Gods," is a paradise that boasts diverse landscapes, lush greenery, pristine beaches, and a rich cultural heritage. Its geography is as captivating as its culture, offering travelers a wide array of experiences. From tranquil coastal areas to breathtaking mountains, this guide will take you on an in-depth journey through the various regions and geographical features that make Bali a truly remarkable destination.

### Overview of Bali's Geography:

Bali is part of Indonesia and is located between the islands of Java and Lombok. It spans approximately 5,780 square kilometers (2,230 square miles) and is characterized by its volcanic origin, resulting in fertile soils, lush vegetation, and impressive mountain ranges. The island's tropical climate, with distinct wet and dry seasons, further contributes to its diverse landscapes.

### Southern Bali:

1. Kuta, Legian, and Seminyak: These areas are known for their vibrant nightlife, bustling beaches, and shopping districts. Kuta Beach is a favorite spot for surfers and sunbathers alike.

2. Jimbaran: Famous for its seafood restaurants on the beach, Jimbaran offers stunning sunset views and a more relaxed atmosphere.

3. Nusa Dua: This luxurious resort area boasts pristine beaches, golf courses, and high-end hotels. It's a haven for those seeking relaxation and upscale amenities.

**Central Bali:**

1. Ubud: Nestled in the heart of Bali, Ubud is a cultural and artistic hub. It's surrounded by terraced rice fields, traditional villages, and numerous art galleries.

Eastern Bali:

1. Candidasa: A quieter coastal area known for its laid-back ambiance, Candidasa offers serene beaches and easy access to cultural sites.

2. Amed and Tulamben: These fishing villages are renowned for their underwater beauty, making them popular destinations for snorkeling and diving.

**Northern Bali:**

1. Lovina: This region is known for its black sand beaches and dolphin watching tours. It offers a more tranquil setting compared to the southern tourist areas.

**Western Bali:**

1. West Bali National Park: Covering a large part of western Bali, this park features diverse ecosystems, including mangroves, rainforests, and coral reefs. It's home to various wildlife species and offers excellent trekking opportunities.

**Mountains and Volcanoes:**

1. Mount Agung: The highest peak in Bali and an active volcano, Mount Agung holds significant spiritual importance. It's a popular destination for hikers, offering stunning sunrise views.

2. Mount Batur: Another active volcano, Mount Batur is known for its trekking trails and the breathtaking sunrise vistas from its summit.

**Rice Terraces:**

1. Tegallalang Rice Terraces: Located near Ubud, these terraces are a UNESCO World Heritage site and showcase Bali's iconic rice cultivation practices.

Underwater Beauty:

1. Coral Reefs: Bali's coastal regions, such as Menjangan Island and Nusa Penida, are known for their vibrant coral reefs, making them prime spots for snorkeling and diving.

Cultural and Natural Landmarks:

1. Besakih Temple: Known as the "Mother Temple," Besakih is the largest and most important temple complex in Bali, located on the slopes of Mount Agung.

2. Tirta Empul Temple: This water temple in Tampaksiring is famous for its holy spring waters used for purification rituals.

3. Uluwatu Temple: Perched atop dramatic cliffs, Uluwatu Temple offers stunning ocean views and traditional Kecak dance performances.

Bali's geography and regions offer a rich tapestry of experiences for travelers. From the bustling beaches of the south to the serene rice terraces of the central highlands, each area presents unique opportunities for exploration and immersion in Bali's culture and natural beauty. Whether you're seeking adventure, relaxation, or cultural insights, the island's diverse landscapes have something to offer every traveler.

## *3.2 Climate and Best Time to Visit*

### Climate in Bali:

Bali's climate is tropical, characterized by distinct wet and dry seasons. Understanding the climate is essential for planning your visit. The dry season, from April to September, is considered the best time to visit as the weather is relatively stable. Rainfall is minimal during these months, and you can expect warm temperatures and plenty of sunshine. The humidity is lower, making it a comfortable time for outdoor activities and exploring the island.

The wet season, from October to March, brings heavier rainfall and higher humidity. While the lush landscapes and lower number of tourists might be appealing, the frequent rain showers can limit your outdoor plans. Be prepared for sudden downpours and occasional flooding in certain areas.

**Best Time to Visit:**

1. April to June: This is arguably the best time to visit Bali. The weather is sunny and dry, and the island is less crowded than during the peak tourist months. It's an excellent time for outdoor activities like surfing, snorkeling, and exploring Bali's natural beauty.

2. July to August: These are the peak tourist months due to school holidays in various countries. While you'll enjoy dry and sunny weather, popular attractions can be quite crowded. Make sure to book accommodations and activities in advance.

3. September: The weather remains pleasant in September, and the crowds start to thin out as schools resume. It's a great time to visit if you want to avoid the peak season rush.

4. October to March: While the wet season brings occasional rain and higher humidity, it's also a time when you can experience the authentic, lush beauty of Bali. The rainfall isn't constant, so you might still enjoy clear days between showers. Just be prepared for some activities to be disrupted by weather conditions.

**Considerations:**

- Crowds: If you prefer a quieter experience, avoid the peak tourist months of July and August. Instead, opt for the shoulder seasons of April to June and September.

- Activities: The dry season is ideal for water activities like surfing, diving, and snorkeling. The wet season is better for enjoying Bali's cultural and indoor attractions.

- Budget: Accommodation and flight prices tend to be higher during the peak season. You might find better deals during the shoulder and low seasons.

- Festivals: Bali celebrates numerous festivals throughout the year. Consider timing your visit with festivals like Galungan and Kuningan

(Balinese Hindu celebrations) or Nyepi (Day of Silence) for a unique cultural experience.

Bali's climate can be unpredictable, so it's wise to pack both light clothing for the warm days and a raincoat or umbrella for unexpected showers. Regardless of the season, Bali offers something special, whether it's the vibrant festivals, stunning beaches, or lush landscapes. Plan your trip based on your interests and preferences to make the most of your Bali experience.

### 3.3 Cultural Etiquette and Customs

Bali, known as the "Island of the Gods," is a stunning destination that boasts not only picturesque landscapes but also a rich and deeply-rooted cultural heritage. As a traveler to this enchanting island, it's crucial to understand and respect the local customs and etiquette to ensure a meaningful and positive experience. Here's an extensive guide to navigating Bali's cultural norms:

**1. Greeting and Politeness:**
Balinese people are warm and hospitable, and greetings are an essential part of their culture. The common greeting is a slight bow with hands placed together in a prayer-like gesture, known as the "salam" or "sampyuh." When addressing someone,

it's customary to use their title and full name, such as "Ibu" (Mrs.) or "Bapak" (Mr.), followed by their given name.

**2. Dress Code:**
Bali is predominantly Hindu, and dressing modestly is crucial to showing respect for the local culture. When visiting temples or religious sites, both men and women should wear a sarong and a sash around the waist. It's also advised to wear appropriate clothing that covers shoulders and knees when outside the beach areas.

**3. Visiting Temples:**
Temples hold immense spiritual significance in Bali. When visiting these sacred sites, remember to wear the appropriate attire and be mindful of your actions. Always approach the temple with a respectful attitude, removing your shoes before entering and avoiding pointing your feet at the shrines or the priest.

**4. Offerings and Ceremony:**
Offerings, called "canang sari," are an integral part of Balinese daily life. These small, intricate baskets are filled with flowers, rice, and incense and are presented to deities and spirits as a gesture of gratitude and respect. If you come across an

offering, it's important not to disturb or step on them.

## 5. Public Displays of Affection:
While Balinese people are generally friendly, public displays of affection, such as hugging or kissing, should be kept to a minimum. Such gestures are considered intimate and are best reserved for private settings.

## 6. Communication and Gestures:
Balinese people value polite and calm communication. Raising your voice or showing anger is highly discouraged, as it's seen as disrespectful. Use your right hand to give or receive objects, as the left hand is considered impolite.

## 7. Photography:
Always ask for permission before taking someone's photo, especially if they are engaged in religious activities or ceremonies. Some temples and locations may have photography restrictions, so it's essential to respect these rules.

## 8. Time and Patience:
Balinese culture operates at a relaxed pace, known as "rubber time." Being patient and flexible when it comes to schedules and plans is important. Rushing

or displaying frustration is counter to the local way of life.

**9. Tipping and Bargaining:**
Tipping is not mandatory in Bali, but it's appreciated, especially in tourist areas. When shopping at markets, bargaining is a common practice, but always do so with a smile and a respectful attitude.

**10. Taboos:**
Avoid touching someone's head, as it's considered the most sacred part of the body. Additionally, pointing your feet at people or religious objects is disrespectful.

Bali's customs and etiquette, you'll not only have a more authentic experience but also foster positive interactions with the local community. Remember, the key to a memorable trip is to approach the island with an open heart and a willingness to embrace its rich cultural heritage.

# CHAPTER 4: Top Destinations

## 4.1 *Exploring Ubud: Cultural Heart of Bali*

Nestled amidst the lush green landscapes of Bali, Ubud is often referred to as the island's cultural heart. This enchanting town offers a captivating blend of artistic expression, traditional Balinese culture, and serene natural beauty. Exploring Ubud is a journey that takes you through ancient temples, vibrant art markets, serene rice terraces, and spiritual experiences. Here's a comprehensive guide to help you make the most of your visit to this cultural gem:

**1. Ubud's Artistic Heritage:**
Ubud has long been a haven for artists, and you'll find countless galleries and studios showcasing everything from traditional paintings to contemporary sculptures. Begin your exploration at the **Puri Lukisan Museum,** which displays a stunning collection of Balinese art. Don't miss the opportunity to engage with local artists, perhaps by taking part in a traditional art class.

**2. Sacred Temples and Spiritual Experiences:**
Ubud is home to several significant temples that offer a glimpse into Bali's deep-rooted spiritual

traditions. The **Ubud Palace,** also known as **Puri Saren Agung,** is not only a cultural landmark but also a venue for traditional dance performances. Another must-visit is the **Ubud Monkey Forest,** a sanctuary that houses ancient temples and playful macaques.

### 3. Ubud's Enchanting Rice Terraces:
The iconic rice terraces surrounding Ubud are a testament to Bali's agricultural heritage. The **Tegallalang Rice Terraces** are renowned for their intricate design and breathtaking views. Take a leisurely stroll through these terraces to immerse yourself in the serene beauty of the landscape and witness local farmers at work.

### 4. Traditional Balinese Performances:
Ubud is known for its vibrant performing arts scene. Attending a traditional dance performance, such as the **Barong Dance** or the **Kecak Fire Dance,** is a captivating way to experience Balinese culture and mythology coming to life through intricate movements and mesmerizing chants.

### 5. Ubud's Ubiquitous Markets:
For a dose of local life and an opportunity to shop for souvenirs, explore the bustling markets of Ubud. The **Ubud Market** is famous for its array of

handicrafts, textiles, jewelry, and art. Remember to practice your bargaining skills and engage in friendly interactions with the local vendors.

**6. Wellness and Healing:**
Ubud has gained international recognition as a wellness destination. The town offers a plethora of yoga and wellness retreats, as well as holistic healing experiences. Explore local spas and centers that offer traditional Balinese massages, healing treatments, and yoga sessions amidst serene natural surroundings.

**7. Gastronomic Delights:**
Ubud's culinary scene is a fusion of traditional Balinese flavors and international cuisine. Don't miss the opportunity to sample authentic dishes such as **Babi Guling** (suckling pig) and **Bebek Betutu** (slow-cooked duck). Explore local warungs (small eateries) for an authentic taste of Balinese cuisine.

**8. Cultural Workshops and Classes:**
Engage in immersive experiences by participating in cultural workshops and classes. Learn traditional Balinese dance, practice yoga with experienced instructors, or discover the art of making offerings and learning about their symbolism.

**9. Eco-Friendly Adventures:**
Ubud's natural surroundings offer a plethora of eco-friendly adventures. Embark on trekking or cycling tours to explore the hidden waterfalls, lush jungles, and vibrant flora that make up the area's stunning landscapes.

**10. Responsible Tourism:**
As you explore Ubud, remember to travel responsibly. Respect local customs and traditions, support local businesses, and minimize your impact on the environment. Participate in community-based initiatives and projects to give back to the community that welcomes you.

Ubud's charm lies not only in its physical beauty but also in the depth of its cultural offerings. Immerse yourself in the town's artistic, spiritual, and natural wonders to truly experience the essence of Bali's cultural heart.

### *4.2 Relaxing in Seminyak and Canggu*

For travelers seeking a blend of relaxation, coastal beauty, and vibrant social scenes, Seminyak and Canggu in Bali are top destinations. These neighboring towns offer a balance of luxury, tranquility, and a laid-back beach lifestyle. From pristine beaches to trendy cafes and upscale boutiques, here's an in-depth guide to help you unwind and rejuvenate in Seminyak and Canggu:

**1. Beachfront Bliss:**
Both Seminyak and Canggu boast stunning beaches that invite you to bask in the sun, take leisurely strolls, or catch the waves. Seminyak Beach offers golden sands and is known for its vibrant beach clubs and stunning sunsets. Echo Beach in Canggu is a surfer's paradise and a great spot to enjoy the coastal breeze.

**2. Luxurious Accommodations:**
Seminyak is renowned for its high-end resorts and luxury villas. Stay in opulent accommodations that offer private pools, spa treatments, and impeccable service. In Canggu, you'll find a mix of boutique hotels, beachfront villas, and cozy guest houses that cater to various budgets.

**3. Spa and Wellness Retreats:**
Both Seminyak and Canggu offer an array of spa and wellness facilities that specialize in traditional Balinese treatments as well as modern therapies. Indulge in massages, facials, and holistic healing sessions to rejuvenate your body and mind.

### 4. Yoga and Mindfulness:
Canggu is known as a hub for yoga and mindfulness enthusiasts. Join a yoga class overlooking the rice fields or the ocean, and explore meditation practices that allow you to find inner peace and serenity.

### 5. Trendy Cafes and Culinary Delights:
Seminyak and Canggu are culinary havens, offering an array of dining options. Explore trendy cafes serving healthy and Instagram-worthy dishes, as well as beachfront restaurants with fresh seafood and international flavors. Be sure to try local Balinese cuisine as well.

### 6. Boutique Shopping:
Indulge in retail therapy at Seminyak's upscale boutiques and Canggu's charming shops. Discover unique clothing, accessories, homeware, and art created by local designers and artisans.

### 7. Sunset Vibes and Nightlife:
Seminyak and Canggu come alive as the sun sets. Enjoy vibrant nightlife at beach clubs and bars where you can sip on cocktails, dance, and enjoy live music with a backdrop of ocean views.

### 8. Exploring Beach Clubs:

Seminyak is known for its beach clubs, such as **Potato Head** and **Ku De Ta,** where you can relax by the pool, savor delicious cuisine, and enjoy a chic atmosphere. Canggu offers beach clubs like **Finn's Beach Club**, perfect for sun-soaked days by the sea.

## 9. Surfing and Adventure:

Canggu is a surfer's paradise with waves suitable for both beginners and experienced surfers. Sign up for surf lessons or rent a board and catch the waves at Echo Beach or Berawa Beach. You can also explore nearby attractions like the Tanah Lot Temple.

## 10. Responsible Tourism:

While unwinding, it's important to practice responsible tourism. Respect local communities, minimize your environmental impact, and support initiatives that promote sustainable practices.

Whether you're seeking luxury and indulgence or a laid-back beach escape, Seminyak and Canggu offer the perfect blend of relaxation and coastal charm. Embrace the tranquility, embrace the vibrant scenes, and find your own balance in these coastal retreats on the beautiful island of Bali.

### *4.3 Stunning Beaches of Kuta and Legian*

Bali's southern coast is adorned with some of the most famous and captivating beaches in the world. Kuta and Legian, located side by side, offer a vibrant mix of sun-soaked sands, thrilling waves, and a lively social scene. From surfing to beachfront relaxation, here's an extensive guide to help you make the most of your time on the stunning beaches of Kuta and Legian:

**1. Kuta Beach: The Iconic Playground:**
Kuta Beach is renowned for its wide stretch of golden sand and legendary sunsets. This beach is perfect for everything from sunbathing and swimming to leisurely strolls and beach games. As the birthplace of Bali's surfing scene, Kuta Beach's waves cater to both beginners and experienced surfers.

**2. Legian Beach: A Tranquil Retreat:**
Adjacent to Kuta, Legian Beach offers a slightly more serene atmosphere. The waves are still ideal for surfing, but the vibe is a bit quieter, making it a great spot for unwinding. With fewer crowds, Legian Beach is an excellent choice for those seeking relaxation and solitude.

**3. Surfing Paradise:**

Both Kuta and Legian are synonymous with surfing. If you're a beginner looking to catch your first wave, many surf schools offer lessons to help you ride the waves safely. For more experienced surfers, the consistent and powerful waves provide an exhilarating challenge.

### 4. Sunset Delights:
Witnessing the sunset over Kuta and Legian beaches is a must-do experience. Find a cozy spot along the shoreline or settle in at one of the beachfront bars to enjoy a breathtaking view as the sun dips below the horizon.

### 5. Water Activities:
Beyond surfing, these beaches offer an array of water activities. Try your hand at parasailing, banana boating, or jet skiing for an adrenaline rush. You can also rent a kayak or stand-up paddleboard to explore the ocean from a different perspective.

### 6. Beachfront Dining:
Kuta and Legian are dotted with beachfront cafes and restaurants that offer a variety of cuisines. Indulge in fresh seafood, tropical cocktails, and local dishes while enjoying the sound of the waves and the ocean breeze.

### 7. Vibrant Nightlife:
As the sun goes down, Kuta and Legian come to life with vibrant nightlife. The beach clubs, bars, and nightclubs along the coastline offer entertainment, live music, and dancing. Experience the lively atmosphere and social scene that make these beaches a favorite among partygoers.

### 8. Family-Friendly Activities:
Families will find plenty of activities to enjoy on these beaches. From building sandcastles to flying kites, the open space is perfect for children to explore and play. The calm waters near the shore are ideal for young swimmers.

### 9. Shopping and Souvenirs:
The beaches of Kuta and Legian are lined with vendors selling everything from souvenirs to local crafts. Take a leisurely stroll along the shoreline and browse for unique items to bring back home as mementos.

### 10. Responsible Beach Enjoyment:
While soaking up the beauty and activities, remember to respect the environment. Dispose of trash properly, avoid disturbing marine life, and practice responsible tourism to preserve the natural beauty of these beaches.

Kuta and Legian beaches offer a captivating blend of relaxation, adventure, and entertainment. Whether you're seeking thrilling waves, breathtaking sunsets, or a vibrant nightlife, these beaches provide an unforgettable experience that captures the essence of Bali's coastal charm.

### 4.4 Tranquility in Uluwatu and Bukit Peninsula

For travelers seeking a serene escape from the bustling crowds of Bali, the Uluwatu region and the Bukit Peninsula offer a tranquil haven. Perched on dramatic cliffs overlooking the Indian Ocean, this area boasts breathtaking vistas, secluded beaches, and a peaceful ambiance. From hidden beaches to cultural wonders, here's an extensive guide to help you find tranquility in Uluwatu and the Bukit Peninsula:

**1. Cliffside Serenity:**
Uluwatu is known for its stunning cliffside locations that offer unobstructed views of the ocean. Many luxury resorts and private villas are perched atop these cliffs, providing an intimate and serene setting for relaxation.

**2. Uluwatu Temple: A Spiritual Gem:**

The **Uluwatu Temple**, perched on a steep cliff, is one of Bali's six key temples. This iconic site not only offers cultural and architectural wonders but also presents a perfect vantage point to witness mesmerizing sunsets over the ocean.

### 3. Secluded Beaches:
The Bukit Peninsula is home to some of Bali's most secluded and pristine beaches. Explore hidden gems such as **Pandawa Beach, Balangan Beach,** and **Green Bowl Beach** to bask in solitude and admire the rugged beauty of the coastline.

### 4. Surfing Nirvana:
Uluwatu and the Bukit Peninsula are renowned for their world-class surfing breaks. Intermediate and advanced surfers can challenge themselves with the waves at **Uluwatu Beach** and **Padang Padang Beach,** while beginners can find more forgiving waves at **Dreamland Beach.**

### 5. Clifftop Bars and Restaurants:
Indulge in culinary delights while taking in panoramic ocean views. Many clifftop bars and restaurants in Uluwatu and the Bukit Peninsula offer a serene atmosphere to savor local and international cuisines.

### 6. Sunset Experiences:
As the sun sets, the Bukit Peninsula becomes a magical place. Witness the sky ablaze with colors as you stand on the cliffs or the beaches, capturing unforgettable moments as the sun dips beneath the horizon.

### 7. Yoga Retreats:
Uluwatu and the Bukit Peninsula offer an array of yoga retreats and wellness centers. Immerse yourself in rejuvenating practices, meditation, and holistic therapies amidst the tranquil surroundings.

### 8. Ocean Adventures:
Embark on ocean adventures such as snorkeling, scuba diving, and stand-up paddleboarding. Discover vibrant marine life and underwater landscapes in the clear waters around the Bukit Peninsula.

### 9. Cultural Performances:
Experience the captivating Kecak dance performance at the **Uluwatu Temple,** where the rhythmic chants and mesmerizing movements tell the story of the Ramayana epic against the backdrop of the setting sun.

**10. Nature Treks and Exploration:**
Explore the rugged terrain and lush landscapes of the Bukit Peninsula through nature treks. Discover hidden viewpoints, explore local villages, and immerse yourself in the natural beauty of the area.

**11. Responsible Travel:**
While seeking tranquility, it's important to practice responsible tourism. Respect local customs, minimize your environmental impact, and support initiatives that conserve the area's natural beauty.

Uluwatu and the Bukit Peninsula offer a retreat from the hustle and bustle of Bali's more touristy areas. Whether you're in search of breathtaking views, secluded beaches, or cultural experiences, this region invites you to unwind and embrace the serene beauty of Bali's southern coastline.

### *4.5 Lovina: North Bali's Hidden Gem*

Tucked away on the tranquil northern coast of Bali, Lovina is a hidden gem that offers a refreshing escape from the island's bustling tourist hotspots. This serene coastal town is known for its black sand beaches, dolphin watching, and laid-back atmosphere. From sunrise boat rides to vibrant coral reefs, here's an extensive guide to help you discover the enchanting beauty of Lovina:

## 1. Black Sand Beaches:
Unlike the golden sands of Bali's southern coast, Lovina's beaches are adorned with unique black volcanic sand. Take leisurely strolls along the shore, enjoy the calming sound of the waves, and immerse yourself in the peaceful ambiance.

## 2. Dolphin Watching:
One of Lovina's most popular attractions is its early morning dolphin watching tours. Board traditional fishing boats and set sail at sunrise to witness playful dolphins frolicking in their natural habitat, creating a magical and unforgettable experience.

## 3. Snorkeling and Diving:
Explore Lovina's vibrant underwater world by indulging in snorkeling or diving adventures. The calm waters of Lovina Bay provide an opportunity to observe colorful coral reefs, marine life, and even the chance to spot dolphins in the deeper waters.

## 4. Banjar Hot Springs:
Just a short drive from Lovina, the **Banjar Hot Springs** offer a unique opportunity to relax in natural thermal pools. The soothing waters, surrounded by lush tropical vegetation, are believed

to have healing properties and provide a serene escape.

### 5. Brahma Vihara Arama:
This Buddhist temple complex is the largest in Bali and is worth a visit for its tranquil atmosphere and stunning views. Explore the intricate architecture, lush gardens, and serene meditation spaces within the temple grounds.

### 6. Air Panas:
Also known as the **Hot Water Temple**, Air Panas is a natural hot spring located nearby. Immerse yourself in the warm, mineral-rich waters while enjoying the surrounding lush landscapes.

### 7. Trekking and Waterfalls:
For those seeking adventure, Lovina offers opportunities for trekking and hiking through the region's lush hills. Discover hidden waterfalls, traverse scenic trails, and witness the stunning vistas of rice terraces and valleys.

### 8. Authentic Local Cuisine:
Indulge in Lovina's local cuisine, which offers a unique blend of Balinese flavors. Try dishes such as **Babi Guling** (suckling pig), **Lawar** (mixed

vegetables and meat), and **Be Siap** (chicken cooked in coconut milk).

### 9. Serene Accommodations:
Lovina boasts a range of accommodations, from boutique resorts to charming guesthouses. Enjoy the tranquility of beachfront stays, lush gardens, and serene surroundings that perfectly complement the town's peaceful ambiance.

### 10. Embracing Local Culture:
Engage with the local community and immerse yourself in their traditions. Visit local markets, interact with friendly villagers, and perhaps even participate in traditional dance or music performances.

### 11. Responsible Exploration:
As you enjoy the beauty of Lovina, remember to practice responsible tourism. Support local businesses, respect the environment, and engage in activities that contribute positively to the community.

Lovina's hidden charm offers a genuine escape from the usual tourist circuits, allowing you to connect with nature, embrace tranquility, and experience the authentic beauty of Bali's north coast. Whether you're seeking dolphin encounters, underwater adventures, or a cultural journey, Lovina promises a peaceful retreat that will leave you refreshed and rejuvenated.

### 4.6 East Bali Adventures: Candidasa and Amed

East Bali is a region of unparalleled beauty and cultural significance, offering a more tranquil and authentic experience compared to the island's busier areas. Candidasa and Amed are two charming destinations that provide a gateway to discovering East Bali's hidden treasures. From underwater wonders to ancient temples, here's an extensive guide to help you embark on unforgettable adventures in Candidasa and Amed:

**1. Candidasa: Coastal Charm and Culture:**
Candidasa is a peaceful coastal town known for its laid-back ambiance and cultural richness. Relax on the pristine white sand beach, where the calm waters make swimming enjoyable. Explore local art galleries, craft shops, and traditional markets to experience the town's artistic flair.

**2. Tirta Gangga: A Water Palace Retreat:**
A short drive from Candidasa, **Tirta Gangga** is a stunning water palace that showcases intricate

architecture and serene pools filled with sacred spring water. Take a leisurely stroll through the gardens, cross the stepping stones, and immerse yourself in a tranquil oasis.

### 3. Pura Lempuyang Luhur: The Gateway to Heaven:

Venture further east to **Pura Lempuyang Luhur,** one of Bali's most iconic temples. The famous "Gates of Heaven" offer a mesmerizing view of Mount Agung and a reflection pond that creates a captivating illusion of floating.

### 4. Amed: Underwater Paradise:

Amed is a tranquil fishing village that has evolved into a paradise for divers and snorkelers. Explore vibrant coral reefs, shipwrecks, and diverse marine life. Amed's relaxed atmosphere provides the perfect setting to unwind after underwater adventures.

### 5. Jemeluk Bay and Japanese Shipwreck:

Snorkel or dive in **Jemeluk Bay** to witness the stunning coral gardens and the hauntingly beautiful **Japanese Shipwreck**. These underwater sites are rich in marine biodiversity and offer an up-close look at the vibrant aquatic world.

### 6. Mount Agung Trekking:
For the adventurous souls, embark on a trek to the summit of **Mount Agung**, Bali's highest volcano. The challenging climb is rewarded with panoramic views of the surrounding landscape and a sense of accomplishment.

### 7. Traditional Salt Farms:
Amed is known for its traditional salt farms, where you can witness the fascinating process of salt production. Observe locals working in the fields and learn about the ancient methods used in this industry.

### 8. Warungs and Culinary Delights:
Indulge in local cuisine at charming warungs (small eateries) in Candidasa and Amed. Try dishes such as **Nasi Campur** (mixed rice) and **Ikan Bakar** (grilled fish) for an authentic taste of Balinese flavors.

### 9. Serene Accommodations:
Both Candidasa and Amed offer a range of accommodations, from budget-friendly guest houses to upscale resorts. Many options provide beachfront or hillside views, allowing you to enjoy the region's natural beauty.

## 10. Embracing Local Traditions:
Engage with the local communities and immerse yourself in their daily life and traditions. Participate in cultural ceremonies, visit local temples, and learn about traditional crafts and activities.

## 11. Responsible Travel:
As you explore Candidasa and Amed, remember to practice responsible tourism. Support local businesses, respect the environment, and engage in activities that contribute positively to the community and the natural surroundings.

Candidasa and Amed offer a serene escape into the heart of East Bali's beauty and culture. Whether you're drawn to underwater explorations, cultural immersions, or natural landscapes, this region invites you to uncover the hidden gems that make East Bali a truly remarkable destination.

# CHAPTER 5: Activities for Everyone

## *5.1 Family-Friendly Attractions*

Bali, with its diverse landscapes and rich culture, is not only a paradise for adults but also a fantastic destination for families. From stunning beaches to interactive cultural experiences, Bali offers a wide array of family-friendly attractions that cater to travelers of all ages. Here's an extensive guide to help you plan a memorable and enjoyable family vacation in Bali:

**1. Beach Adventures:**
Bali's beautiful beaches provide endless opportunities for family fun. Spend sun-soaked days building sandcastles, playing beach games, and splashing in the waves. Popular family-friendly beaches include **Nusa Dua Beach, Sanur Beach,** and the calm waters of **Jimbaran Bay.**

**2. Water Parks:**
Bali is home to several water parks that offer a mix of exhilarating slides, lazy rivers, and kid-friendly play areas. **Waterbom Bali** in Kuta is a top choice, providing a safe and exciting environment for children and adults alike.

**3. Bali Safari and Marine Park:**

Embark on a wildlife adventure at the **Bali Safari and Marine Park** in Gianyar. The park offers close encounters with animals from around the world, as well as thrilling safari rides and animal shows.

**4. Bali Bird Park:**
Discover the fascinating world of avian diversity at the **Bali Bird Park** in Gianyar. Children can learn about various bird species through interactive exhibits and bird shows set amidst lush gardens.

**5. Bali Treetop Adventure Park:**
Located in Bedugul, the **Bali Treetop Adventure Park** provides a thrilling experience for families. Navigate through tree canopies on rope courses, zip lines, and suspension bridges while surrounded by beautiful nature.

**6. Turtle Conservation Centers:**
Visit the **Turtle Conservation and Education Center** in Serangan or **Turtle Island** in Tanjung Benoa. These centers offer educational opportunities for children to learn about sea turtles and their conservation efforts.

**7. Bali Zoo:**

The **Bali Zoo** in Gianyar is another family-friendly attraction where kids can get up close and personal with animals through interactive exhibits and animal encounters.

## 8. Balinese Cultural Shows:
Expose your family to the rich Balinese culture through traditional dance performances such as the **Barong Dance** or **Kecak Dance**. These captivating shows are not only entertaining but also provide insights into local mythology and traditions.

## 9. Ubud Monkey Forest:
Explore the **Ubud Monkey Forest,** a sanctuary where families can observe playful macaques in their natural habitat. The lush surroundings make it an educational and enjoyable outing.

## 10. Family Cooking Classes:
Engage in a family cooking class to learn how to prepare authentic Balinese dishes. Many cooking schools offer hands-on experiences that allow children to learn about local ingredients and cooking techniques.

## 11. Surfing Lessons:

Bali's waves cater to both beginners and experienced surfers. Consider enrolling the family in a surfing lesson where everyone can learn to ride the waves together.

**12. Responsible Travel:**
Teach your children about responsible tourism by respecting local customs, minimizing waste, and participating in community-based activities that support the local economy.

Bali's family-friendly attractions promise a vacation filled with adventure, culture, and bonding experiences. Whether you're exploring wildlife, enjoying the beaches, or immersing yourselves in the local culture, Bali offers a diverse range of activities that will create cherished memories for your entire family.

### *5.1.1 Waterbom Bali*

Nestled in the heart of Kuta, Waterbom Bali stands as one of the island's premier water parks and a favorite among visitors seeking fun and excitement. With a wide array of water slides, attractions, and serene landscapes, Waterbom Bali offers a perfect blend of adrenaline-pumping adventures and relaxing respites. Whether you're traveling with family, friends, or seeking a solo adventure, this comprehensive guide will help you make the most of your visit to Waterbom Bali.

**1. Attractions for All Ages:**
Waterbom Bali boasts a variety of attractions catering to all age groups. From heart-pounding slides like the **Smash Down 2.0** and the **Python** to the **Lazy River** and the **Funtastic** play area for younger visitors, there's something for everyone.

**2. The Climax:**
One of Waterbom Bali's most iconic rides, **The Climax,** provides an exhilarating drop from an 18.5-meter tower. This high-speed slide offers an adrenaline rush that's not for the faint-hearted.

**3. Flow Rider:**
Surfing enthusiasts can catch their waves on the **Flow Rider**, an artificial wave pool that replicates the experience of riding ocean waves. Both beginners and experienced surfers can enjoy the challenge of balancing on this endless wave.

**4. Constrictor:**
The **Constrictor** slide is a unique experience where riders traverse through twists and turns in a series of enclosed tubes, offering a thrilling adventure of darkness and excitement.

**5. Relaxation Zones:**
For those seeking relaxation, Waterbom Bali offers serene spaces like the **Lazy River,** where you can leisurely float on tubes through a gentle water course. Relax by the **Cabana Area** where you can unwind in comfort and style.

**6. F&B and Amenities:**
The water park offers a variety of food and beverage options to satisfy your cravings. From local Balinese dishes to international cuisine, you'll find something to suit your taste buds. There are also well-equipped changing rooms, lockers, and shower facilities for your convenience.

**7. Green Initiatives:**
Waterbom Bali is committed to environmental sustainability. The park employs eco-friendly practices such as water recycling, waste reduction, and energy-efficient operations, showcasing a responsible approach to tourism.

**8. Safety and Cleanliness:**
Safety is a top priority at Waterbom Bali. Lifeguards are stationed throughout the park, and all attractions adhere to strict safety guidelines. The

park is well-maintained, ensuring a clean and hygienic environment for visitors.

### 9. Booking and Tips:
It's recommended to book tickets in advance to avoid long lines. Consider arriving early to make the most of your day. Don't forget essentials like sunscreen, swimwear, and comfortable footwear.

### 10. Family-Friendly Experience:
Waterbom Bali is family-oriented, with attractions suitable for various age groups. The **Kiddy Park** is designed for young children, ensuring that the entire family can enjoy a day of fun together.

### 11. Responsible Enjoyment:
As you enjoy the thrills and relaxation at Waterbom Bali, remember to practice responsible tourism by disposing of trash properly, respecting the park's rules, and minimizing your impact on the environment.

Waterbom Bali is more than just a water park; it's an immersive experience that offers adventure, relaxation, and quality family time. With its world-class facilities, diverse attractions, and commitment to sustainability, Waterbom Bali promises a day of unforgettable fun for visitors of all ages.

### *5.1.2 Bali Safari and Marine Park*

Nestled in the heart of Gianyar, the Bali Safari and Marine Park is a captivating haven that allows visitors to immerse themselves in the wonders of the animal kingdom. This sprawling wildlife attraction offers a unique blend of safari experiences, interactive animal encounters, and conservation efforts. Whether you're traveling with family, friends, or embarking on a solo adventure, this comprehensive guide will help you make the most of your visit to the Bali Safari and Marine Park.

1. Safari Journey:
The highlight of the park is the **Safari Journey**, an open-air tram ride that takes you through carefully designed habitats that mimic the natural environments of various animals. Get up close to majestic lions, elephants, zebras, and more, while experienced guides provide fascinating insights about each species.

**2. Animal Encounters:**
Bali Safari and Marine Park offers the opportunity for interactive animal encounters. Feed and interact

with friendly animals such as elephants, giraffes, and orangutans. The **Elephant Back Safari** allows you to ride on the back of these gentle giants through lush landscapes.

### 3. Freshwater Aquarium:
The park's **Freshwater Aquarium** showcases a diverse array of aquatic life, including tropical fish, turtles, and even piranhas. Educational exhibits provide insights into freshwater ecosystems.

### 4. Marine Park:
The Bali Safari and Marine Park features a Marine Park that introduces you to the vibrant marine life of Indonesia. Witness incredible sea creatures, enjoy dolphin shows, and explore the underwater world through the **Aqua Trek** program.

### 5. Educational Programs:
The park is dedicated to raising awareness about wildlife conservation. Engage in educational programs, animal feeding sessions, and behind-the-scenes tours to learn about the importance of preserving endangered species.

### 6. Night Safari:
For a unique experience, consider participating in the **Night Safari**. Witness the nocturnal behaviors

of animals in their natural habitats, guided by specialized night-vision equipment.

### 7. Cultural Shows:
The Bali Agung Show, performed at the park's state-of-the-art theater, is a theatrical production that showcases the island's rich cultural heritage through dance and drama.

### 8. Petting Zoo:
The **Petting Zoo** is a hit with young visitors, offering a safe space to interact with friendly farm animals and learn about animal care.

### 9. Dining and Amenities:
The park features a variety of dining options serving local and international cuisines. Whether you're craving a quick snack or a full meal, you'll find choices that suit your palate.

### 10. Green Initiatives:
The Bali Safari and Marine Park is committed to eco-friendly practices. The park's initiatives include waste reduction, water conservation, and environmental education.

### 11. Booking and Tips:

It's recommended to book tickets in advance to ensure availability, especially during peak seasons. Wear comfortable clothing, sunscreen, and appropriate footwear for walking.

**12. Responsible Tourism:**
As you engage with the animals and enjoy the park's attractions, remember to respect the animals and follow the park's guidelines for a safe and responsible experience.

The Bali Safari and Marine Park offers an extraordinary opportunity to connect with nature, learn about wildlife conservation, and witness the beauty of various animal species up close. With its commitment to education, conservation, and family-friendly experiences, the park promises a day of unforgettable adventure and discovery.

### *5.1.3 Bali Treetop Adventure Park*

Nestled in the lush landscapes of Bedugul, the Bali Treetop Adventure Park offers an exhilarating experience that combines outdoor adventure with stunning natural beauty. This treetop park boasts a series of thrilling challenges, zip lines, and obstacle courses set high in the trees, providing an exciting day out for visitors of all ages. Whether you're seeking an adrenaline rush, a family-friendly outing, or a unique way to explore Bali's wilderness, this comprehensive guide will help you make the most of your visit to Bali Treetop Adventure Park.

**1. Adventure Courses:**
Bali Treetop Adventure Park offers multiple adventure circuits designed to cater to different ages and skill levels. From the **Squirrel Yellow Circuit** for young adventurers to the **Black Circuit** for the most daring, each course presents a mix of obstacles, swings, and zip lines.

**2. Tarzan Jumps:**
Get your heart racing with the **Tarzan Jumps,** where you swing from a height and release to plunge into a net below. It's an adrenaline-pumping activity that brings out the adventurer in you.

**3. High-Flying Zip Lines:**
The park is known for its thrilling zip lines that let you soar above the treetops and admire the scenic views from new heights. The sensation of gliding through the air is a highlight for many visitors.

**4. Kids' Circuit:**
The park is family-friendly, offering a dedicated **Kids' Circuit** that allows young explorers to have

their own adventure. Parents can supervise from below as children navigate fun challenges.

### 5. Safety First:
Safety is a priority at Bali Treetop Adventure Park. All participants are provided with safety equipment including harnesses and helmets. Trained instructors offer guidance and ensure that proper safety measures are followed.

### 6. Beautiful Natural Setting:
Set amidst the serene Bedugul Botanical Gardens, the park offers a unique perspective of Bali's lush landscapes. The courses take you through towering trees and provide panoramic views of the surrounding environment.

### 7. Booking and Tips:
To ensure availability, it's advisable to book your visit in advance. Wear comfortable clothing, closed-toe shoes, and sunscreen. Lockers are available to store your belongings during the adventure.

### 8. Group Activities:
Bali Treetop Adventure Park is an ideal venue for group activities, team building, and celebrations.

The park offers a range of packages and can accommodate various group sizes.

**9. Eco-Friendly Practices:**
The park follows eco-friendly practices by minimizing impact on the environment and conducting regular checks to ensure the well-being of the trees used for the courses.

**10. Responsible Adventure:**
While enjoying the high-flying fun, remember to respect the natural surroundings and follow the instructions provided by the park's staff to ensure a safe and enjoyable experience.

Bali Treetop Adventure Park offers an exciting blend of outdoor challenges, exhilarating zip lines, and breathtaking views. With its emphasis on safety, family-friendly options, and commitment to providing an eco-friendly adventure, the park promises an unforgettable day of fun and adventure for visitors of all ages.

### *5.2 Romantic Experiences for Couples*

Bali's enchanting landscapes, serene beaches, and rich cultural heritage make it a perfect destination for couples seeking romantic getaways. From idyllic sunsets to private escapes, the island offers a plethora of experiences that cater to romance. Whether you're celebrating an anniversary, honeymoon, or simply looking to kindle the flames of love, this extensive guide will help you create unforgettable romantic memories in Bali.

**1. Sunset at Uluwatu Temple:**
Witness the mesmerizing sunset over the Indian Ocean at **Uluwatu Temple.** The breathtaking views, dramatic cliffs, and the temple's mystical ambiance make for an unforgettable romantic experience.

2. Romantic Beach Dinners:
Indulge in a private beach dinner under the stars. Many resorts offer personalized dining experiences where you can enjoy delectable cuisine while listening to the soothing sounds of the ocean.

**3. Private Villa Stays:**
Escape to a luxurious private villa where you and your partner can revel in seclusion and intimacy. Enjoy your own infinity pool, lush gardens, and stunning views, all while relishing the comfort and privacy of your own space.

**4. Spa Retreats for Couples:**

Relax and rejuvenate with your loved one at one of Bali's renowned spa retreats. Enjoy couples' massages, holistic treatments, and soothing spa rituals set in tranquil surroundings.

### 5. Hot Air Balloon Rides:
Take to the skies in a hot air balloon and enjoy a unique vantage point of Bali's beauty. Glide over rice terraces, coastline, and lush landscapes while sharing the awe-inspiring experience with your partner.

### 6. Romantic Ubud:
Ubud's lush greenery and artistic ambiance provide the perfect backdrop for romance. Explore hand-in-hand through rice fields, visit art galleries, and enjoy intimate dinners at quaint restaurants.

### 7. Hidden Waterfalls:
Embark on a journey to discover Bali's hidden waterfalls. Trek together to enchanting spots like **Tegenungan Waterfall** and revel in the natural beauty of cascading waters and lush surroundings.

### 8. Romantic Boat Rides:
Sail on a traditional Balinese boat or a luxurious yacht and explore Bali's coastline. From snorkeling

in crystal-clear waters to enjoying the sea breeze, a boat ride offers a romantic escape.

## 9. Balinese Dance Performances:
Immerse yourselves in Bali's cultural heritage by attending traditional dance performances. The graceful movements and emotive storytelling create a captivating experience for couples.

## 10. Mount Batur Sunrise Trek:
Embark on an early morning trek up **Mount Batur** to catch the sunrise. The breathtaking views from the summit create an awe-inspiring and unforgettable moment shared with your partner.

## 11. Wine and Dine:
Bali's culinary scene offers an array of romantic dining options. From beachfront seafood feasts to intimate candlelit dinners at upscale restaurants, you'll find the perfect setting to savor delicious cuisine.

## 12. Balinese Cooking Classes:
Embark on a culinary journey together by joining a Balinese cooking class. Learn to prepare traditional dishes and create lasting memories as you share the joy of cooking.

### 13. Dreamy Beach Picnics:
Arrange a dreamy beach picnic complete with soft sands, comfortable cushions, and a gourmet spread. Enjoy the serene setting as you share a meal and connect with your partner.

### 14. Floating Breakfasts:
Experience indulgence with a floating breakfast served in your private pool. This lavish option allows you to begin your day with culinary delights in the most romantic of settings.

### 15. Responsible Romance:
As you indulge in these romantic experiences, remember to be responsible tourists. Respect local customs, minimize environmental impact, and leave only footprints behind.

Bali's romantic offerings extend beyond its stunning landscapes, inviting couples to create memories that will be cherished forever. Whether you're seeking adventure, relaxation, or cultural exploration, Bali's romantic experiences are sure to ignite the sparks of love and create moments that will last a lifetime.

### *5.2.1 Sunset at Tanah Lot Temple*

Bali's Tanah Lot Temple stands as an iconic symbol of the island's spiritual heritage and natural beauty. Perched on a rocky outcrop amidst the Indian Ocean, this ancient sea temple is renowned for its breathtaking sunsets that paint the sky with hues of gold and crimson. A visit to Tanah Lot offers an opportunity to witness a magical sunset backdrop, steeped in Balinese culture and serenity. This comprehensive guide will help you make the most of your visit to experience the captivating sunset at Tanah Lot Temple.

**1. The Temple's Significance:**
Tanah Lot Temple holds great spiritual significance in Balinese culture. It is one of Bali's seven sea temples, each believed to guard the island from evil spirits and offer blessings for prosperity and harmony.

**2. Timing and Arriving Early:**
Arriving early allows you to explore the temple grounds, discover the ancient shrines, and learn about the history and rituals associated with Tanah Lot. The area can get crowded as sunset approaches, so an early arrival ensures a more peaceful experience.

### 3. The Majestic Sunset:
As the sun begins its descent, the temple's silhouette against the fiery sky creates a stunning visual spectacle. The colors reflect off the ocean, transforming the landscape into a surreal masterpiece.

### 4. The Holy Snake:
Keep an eye out for the sacred sea snakes that inhabit the caves around Tanah Lot Temple. These snakes are believed to be guardians of the temple and are a significant aspect of its mystique.

### 5. Pura Batu Bolong:
Adjacent to Tanah Lot Temple is **Pura Batu Bolong,** a smaller sea temple with an arched rock formation. This temple offers another picturesque viewpoint to enjoy the sunset.

### 6. Sunset Photography:
Photography enthusiasts will be delighted by the opportunity to capture the temple against the backdrop of the setting sun. The changing colors and dramatic scenery make for unforgettable photo opportunities.

### 7. Cultural Performances:

As the sun sets, Tanah Lot comes alive with traditional Balinese music and dance performances. The rhythmic melodies and graceful movements add an extra layer of enchantment to the experience.

**8. Savor Local Flavors:**
After witnessing the sunset, explore the surrounding area where you'll find local stalls offering Balinese snacks and refreshments. Savor traditional flavors while relishing the tranquil atmosphere.

**9. Balinese Blessings:**
Immerse yourself in the spiritual essence of Tanah Lot by receiving a **melukat** (holy water blessing) from the temple's priests. This ritual is believed to cleanse and purify the soul.

**10. Responsible Visit:**
Respect the temple's cultural significance by dressing modestly, adhering to the rules, and being mindful of your behavior. Carry out your visit with reverence for the sacred site.

**11. Unique Night Visits:**
Consider visiting Tanah Lot during its special **Piodalan** (temple anniversary) ceremonies, which

usually occur during sunset. These ceremonies offer a unique chance to witness traditional rituals and immerse yourself in Balinese spirituality.

The sunset at Tanah Lot Temple is a timeless experience that merges natural beauty with spiritual reverence. As the sun dips below the horizon and paints the sky with its vivid colors, you'll find yourself captivated by the tranquility and magic that surround this ancient sea temple.

### *5.2.2 Romantic Beach Dinners*

Bali's picturesque beaches, soothing ocean waves, and breathtaking sunsets provide an ideal backdrop for romantic moments. One of the most enchanting ways to celebrate love is through a romantic beach dinner. With toes in the sand and the sound of the waves as your soundtrack, Bali offers a plethora of options for couples seeking intimate and memorable dining experiences. This comprehensive guide will help you plan an unforgettable romantic beach dinner in Bali.

### 1. Choosing the Perfect Spot:

Bali boasts an array of beaches where you can enjoy a romantic dinner. From the famous **Jimbaran Bay** to more secluded spots like **Canggu Beach**, the choice depends on your preference for privacy, ambiance, and views.

## 2. Sunset or Starlit:
Decide whether you want to enjoy your romantic beach dinner against the backdrop of a stunning sunset or under a canopy of stars. Both options offer unique atmospheres that cater to different romantic preferences.

## 3. Private Dining Setup:
Many resorts and restaurants in Bali offer private beach dining setups that include comfortable seating, elegant decor, and personalized service. From comfortable cushions to torches and lanterns, the setups are designed to enhance the romantic ambiance.

## 4. Culinary Delights:
Indulge in a delectable culinary experience tailored to your preferences. Bali's dining scene offers a range of international and local cuisine, allowing you to savor dishes that match your taste.

## 5. Seafood Feast:
Bali's coastal charm is best complemented by a seafood feast. Try fresh catches of the day,

succulent prawns, grilled fish, and other ocean delights prepared with Balinese flavors.

### 6. Personalized Menus:
Many venues offer the opportunity to create a personalized menu for your romantic dinner. This allows you to select dishes you both love and cater to any dietary restrictions.

### 7. Serenade and Entertainment:
Enhance the romantic experience by arranging for live music, a local serenade, or cultural performances that serenade you during your meal.

### 8. Sunset Gazing:
If you're opting for a sunset beach dinner, enjoy the anticipation of the sun sinking below the horizon. The changing colors of the sky create a mesmerizing backdrop for your evening.

### 9. Stargazing:
For starlit dinners, the clear Balinese night sky provides an opportunity for stargazing and sharing quiet moments under the celestial canopy.

### 10. Beach Bonfires:
Consider arranging for a beach bonfire after your dinner. Sitting by the warmth of the fire, sharing

stories and laughter, creates an intimate and cozy atmosphere.

## 11. Booking and Planning:
Reserve your romantic beach dinner in advance, especially during peak seasons. Communicate your preferences, dietary restrictions, and any special requests to ensure your evening is tailored to perfection.

## 12. Capturing Memories:
Consider hiring a photographer to capture the magical moments of your romantic beach dinner. These photographs will serve as cherished mementos of your time together.

## 13. Responsible Romance:
Respect the beach environment by cleaning up after your dinner, adhering to local regulations, and minimizing your impact on the natural surroundings.

A romantic beach dinner in Bali is more than just a meal; it's an experience that allows you to connect, celebrate, and create lasting memories with your loved one. With the ocean as your backdrop and the stars as your witnesses, these dinners embody the essence of romance and offer a chance to revel in the beauty of love.

### 5.2.3 Spa and Wellness Retreats

Bali's serene landscapes, ancient healing traditions, and tranquil ambiance make it a sought-after destination for spa and wellness retreats. Whether you're seeking relaxation, rejuvenation, or holistic healing, the island offers a wide array of luxurious spas and wellness centers that cater to your well-being. This comprehensive guide will help you navigate the world of spa and wellness retreats in Bali and make the most of your rejuvenating journey.

**1. Ubud: The Wellness Hub:**
Ubud, often referred to as Bali's spiritual heart, is a haven for wellness seekers. The town is home to numerous wellness retreats, yoga centers, and holistic healing spaces.

**2. Traditional Balinese Healing:**
Experience the magic of traditional Balinese healing therapies, including **Balinese massages,** herbal baths, and energy healing treatments. These therapies are deeply rooted in local customs and ancient knowledge.

### 3. Luxury Resorts and Spas:
Bali boasts an array of luxury resorts and spas that offer world-class wellness experiences. From serene oceanfront sanctuaries to lush jungle hideaways, you'll find a variety of options that cater to your preferences.

### 4. Yoga and Meditation Retreats:
Bali is a paradise for yoga enthusiasts. Join yoga and meditation retreats that blend physical practice, mindfulness, and spiritual growth in tranquil settings.

### 5. Ayurveda Retreats:
Discover the principles of Ayurveda, an ancient Indian system of holistic healing, through specialized retreats that focus on balancing mind, body, and spirit.

### 6. Holistic Healing:
Explore holistic healing practices such as **sound therapy**, crystal healing, and chakra balancing to restore harmony and enhance your overall well-being.

### 7. Signature Treatments:
Many spas offer signature treatments inspired by Balinese traditions. From soothing **flower baths**

to invigorating **jamu scrubs**, these treatments offer a unique and authentic experience.

### 8. Spa Facilities and Amenities:
Spa and wellness retreats often include facilities such as saunas, steam rooms, pools, and relaxation lounges. These amenities enhance your wellness journey and allow for complete rejuvenation.

### 9. Organic and Healthy Cuisine:
Embrace a holistic approach to well-being by indulging in organic and healthy cuisine. Many wellness retreats offer farm-to-table dining experiences that nourish your body from the inside out.

### 10. Mindfulness Workshops:
Participate in mindfulness workshops that teach techniques for stress reduction, relaxation, and living in the present moment. These workshops provide tools you can take back home.

### 11. Responsible Wellness:
When choosing wellness retreats, opt for centers that promote sustainable practices and respect the local environment. Engage in activities that contribute positively to the community.

### 12. Planning and Booking:
Research the various spa and wellness retreats available in Bali to find one that aligns with your preferences. Plan your itinerary to include a mix of spa treatments, wellness activities, and leisurely exploration.

### 13. Personalized Retreats:
Some wellness centers offer personalized retreats that allow you to customize your experience based on your individual goals and preferences.

A spa and wellness retreat in Bali is not just a vacation; it's a transformative journey that rejuvenates your body, mind, and soul. As you indulge in ancient therapies, embrace holistic practices, and immerse yourself in the island's natural beauty, you'll find yourself renewed and invigorated, ready to embrace life with a sense of balance and well-being.

# CHAPTER 6: Exploring Nature and Adventure

## 6.1 *Mount Batur Sunrise Trek*

Bali, known for its stunning landscapes and rich cultural experiences, offers travelers an unforgettable adventure: the Mount Batur Sunrise Trek. This experience allows you to witness a breathtaking sunrise from the summit of an active volcano, providing not only an awe-inspiring visual spectacle but also a rewarding physical challenge. In this comprehensive travel guide, we'll delve into the details of the Mount Batur Sunrise Trek, ensuring you're well-prepared for this remarkable journey.

Mount Batur, standing at 1,717 meters above sea level, is one of Bali's most iconic and accessible volcanoes. Nestled in the Kintamani Highlands, this active volcano offers a relatively moderate trek that appeals to both seasoned hikers and beginners. The highlight of the trek is undoubtedly the sunrise view, which paints the sky with hues of pink, orange, and gold, illuminating the surrounding landscape.

**Preparing for the Trek:**

1. Fitness Level: While the trek is considered moderate, a reasonable level of fitness is recommended. Regular exercise and cardiovascular activities can help prepare your body for the climb.

2. Clothing and Gear: Wear comfortable hiking attire, sturdy shoes with good grip, and layered clothing to adapt to the changing temperatures. Don't forget a hat, sunglasses, and sunscreen for sun protection.

3. Timing: Most treks commence in the early hours of the morning to reach the summit in time for sunrise. Depending on your starting point, the trek typically takes around two to three hours.

**The Trekking Experience:**
1. Starting Point: The most common starting point for the trek is the Toya Bungkah village. Guides are usually required for this trek, and they can be hired at the starting point. The guides are not only knowledgeable about the trail but also enhance the overall experience with their insights.

2. Trail Terrain: The trek is a mix of well-marked paths and rocky terrain. As you ascend, you'll pass through lush forests, volcanic sand, and volcanic

rocks. The trail can be challenging at times, with steep sections that require steady footing.

3. Sunrise Spectacle: The ascent to the summit is timed to reach the top before dawn. As you near the peak, the anticipation builds, and witnessing the sunrise from this vantage point is truly magical. The view of Lake Batur and Mount Agung in the distance adds to the grandeur.

**Top Tips for a Successful Trek:**
1. Hydration and Snacks: Carry enough water to stay hydrated and energy-boosting snacks to keep you fueled throughout the trek.

2. Camera: Don't forget your camera or smartphone to capture the mesmerizing sunrise and the stunning vistas.

3. Guides: While some experienced trekkers might attempt the trail independently, hiring a guide is recommended for navigation, safety, and enriching your understanding of the area.

The Mount Batur Sunrise Trek is an unforgettable adventure that combines physical exertion with a magnificent natural spectacle. It's a remarkable experience that should be on every traveler's Bali itinerary. As you stand at the summit, taking in the beauty of the sunrise, the serenity of the landscape, and the sense of accomplishment, you'll realize that this journey is more than just a trek; it's an opportunity to connect with nature and create lasting memories. So, lace up your hiking boots, embrace the challenge, and embark on a journey that will stay with you long after you've left the slopes of Mount Batur.

### 6.2 Sacred Monkey Forest Sanctuary

Immerse yourself in the mystical allure of Bali's Sacred Monkey Forest Sanctuary, a haven where nature, culture, and spirituality harmoniously converge. Nestled within the heart of Ubud, this enchanting sanctuary offers travelers a unique opportunity to connect with nature, observe playful macaques in their habitat, and explore sacred temples. In this comprehensive travel guide, we'll delve into the intricacies of the Sacred Monkey Forest Sanctuary, unveiling its cultural significance, natural wonders, and practical tips for a fulfilling visit.

The Sacred Monkey Forest Sanctuary, locally known as "Mandala Suci Wenara Wana," is a lush 27-acre preserve in the Ubud region of Bali. Established as both a spiritual and conservation space, it's home to over 700 Balinese long-tailed macaques (Macaca fascicularis) and houses three ancient temples - Pura Dalem Agung Padangtegal, Pura Beji, and Pura Prajapati.

**Cultural Significance:**
1. Spiritual Connection: The sanctuary is an integral part of Balinese Hinduism. The three temples within its boundaries are actively used by local worshippers, adding an air of sacredness to the forest.

2. Symbolism: The macaques are considered sacred and are believed to be protectors of the area. They hold a spiritual significance that's deeply woven into the fabric of Balinese culture and mythology.

**Exploring the Sanctuary:**
1. Natural Beauty: As you step into the sanctuary, you're greeted by a lush landscape of towering trees, ancient stone sculptures, and meandering pathways. The atmosphere is serene, creating a tranquil space to escape the bustling world outside.

2. Macaque Interaction: The highlight of a visit is undoubtedly the opportunity to observe and interact with the macaques. While they're accustomed to human presence, it's essential to

follow guidelines provided by the sanctuary to ensure both your safety and the welfare of the monkeys.

3. Temple Exploration: The three temples are architectural marvels, each with its unique significance. Pura Dalem Agung Padangtegal, situated in the heart of the forest, is dedicated to Lord Shiva and features intricate carvings and spiritual relics.

**Tips for a Fulfilling Visit:**
1. Respect the Monkeys: While the macaques are accustomed to humans, it's important to maintain a respectful distance, avoid sudden movements, and not feed them, as it can alter their behavior.

2. Clothing: Dress modestly as a sign of respect for the sacredness of the site. Wear appropriate clothing that covers your shoulders and knees.

3. Valuables: Keep your belongings secure, as the curious macaques might attempt to investigate bags and pockets.

4. Guides: Consider hiring a local guide at the entrance for insightful information about the

sanctuary's history, cultural significance, and the monkeys' behavior.

**Environmental and Conservation Efforts:**
The Sacred Monkey Forest Sanctuary also plays a vital role in conserving the region's biodiversity. The lush forest is a habitat for various plant species, birds, and other animals, creating a delicate ecosystem that requires protection.

The Sacred Monkey Forest Sanctuary is more than a tourist attraction; it's a realm where spirituality, culture, and nature intertwine. As you explore its pathways, interact with its inhabitants, and absorb the serene ambiance, you'll come to understand the essence of Balinese life and beliefs. This sanctuary invites you to experience the enchantment of a world where monkeys and humans coexist amidst ancient temples and lush foliage. So, venture into this mystical haven, embrace its beauty, and leave with a deeper appreciation for Bali's rich cultural and natural heritage.

### *6.3 Scenic Rice Terraces of Tegalalang*

Embark on a journey through the artistic landscapes of Bali's Tegalalang Rice Terraces, where nature and human creativity intertwine to create a breathtaking tapestry of lush green fields.

Located in the heart of the island, these iconic terraced rice paddies offer travelers a glimpse into Bali's agricultural heritage, stunning vistas, and a serene escape from the bustling world. In this comprehensive travel guide, we'll delve into the allure of the Tegalalang Rice Terraces, exploring their history, significance, and practical tips for an immersive experience.

The Tegalalang Rice Terraces are an iconic agricultural marvel located approximately 10 kilometers north of Ubud, Bali. Carved into the contours of the landscape, these terraces have been cultivated for centuries, shaping a harmonious relationship between humans and nature.

**Cultural Significance:**
1. Rice Cultivation: Rice is not only a staple in Balinese cuisine but also an integral part of the island's culture and economy. The terraces represent the ancient Subak irrigation system, a UNESCO World Heritage practice that showcases the Balinese philosophy of "Tri Hita Karana" - the harmonious relationship between humans, nature, and the divine.

2. Artistic Expression: The terraces themselves are an artistic expression, showcasing the ingenuity and

creativity of the Balinese people. The patterns and curves of the rice fields are both practical and visually stunning.

**Exploring the Terraces:**
1. Visual Delight: As you approach the Tegalalang Rice Terraces, the view is nothing short of awe-inspiring. Cascading layers of rice fields hug the slopes, creating an intricate mosaic of emerald hues that seem to stretch into infinity.

2. Rice Farming: Witnessing the traditional method of rice farming is a mesmerizing experience. Depending on the time of year, you might see farmers planting, tending, or harvesting the rice, offering a unique insight into their way of life.

3. Cultural Interaction: While exploring the terraces, you might encounter local farmers who are often open to sharing their knowledge about rice cultivation and their daily routines.

**Tips for an Immersive Experience:**
1. Best Time to Visit: The early morning hours or late afternoon provide the best lighting for photography and a more tranquil atmosphere. Avoid midday as the sun can be intense.

2. Footwear: Wear comfortable and sturdy footwear as the paths through the terraces can be uneven and muddy.

3. Exploration: Take your time to explore the terraces on foot. Wander along the narrow paths, cross the bamboo bridges, and soak in the panoramic views from different vantage points.

**Environmental and Sustainable Practices:**
The preservation of the Tegalalang Rice Terraces is crucial for both cultural heritage and environmental sustainability. Several local initiatives aim to promote responsible tourism and maintain the integrity of the landscape.

The Tegalalang Rice Terraces are a testament to Bali's intricate relationship with nature and its commitment to preserving cultural legacies. As you wander through these verdant landscapes, you'll not only capture stunning photographs but also gain a deeper understanding of the island's agricultural heritage and the profound connection between humans and the land. So, venture into this living masterpiece, absorb the serenity, and leave with memories of a visual symphony that will linger in your heart long after you've left the terraced fields behind.

## 6.4 Diving and Snorkeling in Menjangan

Explore the underwater wonders of Bali's Menjangan Island, a paradise for divers and snorkelers seeking to immerse themselves in a vibrant marine ecosystem. Situated within the protected boundaries of West Bali National Park, Menjangan Island offers crystal-clear waters, thriving coral reefs, and an abundance of marine life. In this comprehensive travel guide, we'll dive into the depths of diving and snorkeling in Menjangan Island, unveiling its underwater treasures, practical tips, and the magic that lies beneath the waves.

Menjangan Island, known as "Deer Island," is a small, uninhabited gem located off the northwestern coast of Bali. Its remote location and protected status have preserved its marine biodiversity, making it a haven for both experienced divers and novice snorkelers.

**Diving Experience:**
1. Diverse Dive Sites: Menjangan Island boasts a variety of dive sites, each offering unique experiences. The Coral Garden is renowned for its colorful corals and reef fish, while the Eel Garden is named after the abundant eels that inhabit the area.

2. Marine Life: Prepare to be mesmerized by the kaleidoscope of marine life. Encounter schools of vibrant fish, graceful turtles, and intriguing critters like seahorses and ghost pipefish. The clear waters offer excellent visibility, enhancing your chances of spotting these fascinating creatures.

3. Underwater Topography: The underwater landscape is equally captivating, with steep walls, caves, and overhangs. These formations are draped in vibrant corals, creating a stunning backdrop for your underwater adventure.

**Snorkeling Experience:**
1. Accessible Beauty: Snorkelers can also relish Menjangan's underwater beauty without the need for extensive equipment or certifications. The shallow reefs close to the shore are teeming with marine life, making it an ideal location for families and those new to snorkeling.

2. Snorkeling Spots: Sites like Coral Garden and Temple Wall offer fantastic snorkeling opportunities. Witness the rich marine life up close as you float over vibrant corals and interact with curious fish.

**Practical Tips:**

1. Reef Conservation: Practice responsible diving and snorkeling by avoiding contact with corals and marine life. Respect the marine environment to ensure its preservation for future generations.

2. Guided Tours: Consider booking a guided diving or snorkeling tour with local operators who are familiar with the area's currents, marine life, and safety protocols.

3. Season: The best time to visit Menjangan Island for diving and snorkeling is during the dry season (April to October) when visibility is at its peak.

4. Safety: Prioritize safety by ensuring your gear is in good condition, following guidelines provided by dive/snorkel operators, and being mindful of your personal comfort level in the water.

**Environmental Awareness:**
Conservation efforts play a pivotal role in maintaining the pristine marine environment of Menjangan Island. Responsible tourism practices and marine park regulations contribute to the protection of its delicate ecosystem.

Diving and snorkeling in Menjangan Island is a gateway to a world of underwater marvels. Whether you're a seasoned diver or a beginner, the island's pristine waters and thriving marine life will leave you awestruck. As you descend into the depths or float gently on the surface, you'll be entranced by the vibrant colors, intricate formations, and the harmony of life beneath the waves. So, dive into this aquatic haven, let the currents carry you, and emerge with memories of an underwater adventure that will stay with you forever.

### 6.5 *Water Sports in Nusa Dua*

Unleash your inner adventurer and make a splash in the aquatic playground of Nusa Dua, Bali. With its pristine beaches, clear blue waters, and an array of exciting water sports, Nusa Dua beckons travelers seeking thrilling experiences on the ocean's surface. From heart-pounding activities to serene pursuits, this comprehensive travel guide will immerse you in the world of water sports in Nusa Dua, showcasing its diversity, safety measures, and the adrenaline-pumping joy that awaits.

Nusa Dua, located on the southeastern coast of Bali, is renowned for its luxurious resorts and stunning coastline. But beyond its serene beauty lies a treasure trove of water sports opportunities, catering to both adrenaline junkies and those seeking more relaxed pursuits.

**Adventurous Water Sports:**
1. Parasailing: Soar high above the waves as a parachute lifts you into the sky, offering panoramic views of the coastline and the vast ocean expanse.

2. Jet Skiing: Experience the thrill of speed as you navigate the waves on a jet ski, feeling the wind in your hair and the sea spray on your skin.

3. Banana Boat Ride: Hold on tight as you ride a banana-shaped inflatable raft, bouncing and gliding over the waves with laughter and excitement.

4. Flyboarding: Defy gravity as water propels you high into the air on a flyboard, allowing you to perform daring acrobatics and experience the sensation of flight.

**Serene Water Pursuits:**
1. Kayaking: Explore the serene waters at your own pace, paddling through Nusa Dua's calm bays and taking in the coastal scenery.

2. Stand-Up Paddleboarding (SUP): Balance on a paddleboard and glide along the tranquil waters,

enjoying a peaceful workout and the chance to spot marine life beneath you.

3. Snorkeling: Discover the underwater wonders of Nusa Dua by snorkeling in the crystal-clear waters, observing colorful coral reefs and tropical fish.

**Safety and Precautions:**
1. Qualified Operators: Choose reputable water sports operators with trained staff who prioritize safety and adhere to proper equipment maintenance.

2. Life Jackets: Always wear a life jacket, especially if you're participating in activities that involve being on or in the water.

3. Guidance: Follow the instructions of trained guides and instructors to ensure a safe and enjoyable experience.

**Environmental Considerations:**
Responsible tourism is vital in preserving the natural beauty of Nusa Dua's marine environment. Avoid touching or disturbing marine life, and refrain from littering to minimize your ecological footprint.

Nusa Dua's array of water sports offers an exhilarating escape from everyday routines, immersing you in a world of excitement and wonder. Whether you're soaring high above the waves or peacefully paddling through calm waters, the experiences here are a testament to Bali's vibrant coastal allure. So, dive into the adventure, embrace the thrill, and emerge from the waves with memories that will forever remind you of the sheer joy and boundless energy of Nusa Dua's water sports paradise.

# CHAPTER 7: Cultural Immersion

## 7.1 Temples and Sacred Sites

Embark on a spiritual odyssey through Bali's enchanting temples and sacred sites, where ancient traditions, intricate architecture, and serene surroundings converge. Known as the "Island of the Gods," Bali is a realm where spirituality is interwoven with daily life. In this comprehensive travel guide, we'll delve into the realm of Bali's temples and sacred sites, unveiling their significance, diverse offerings, and the profound cultural experiences they offer to travelers.

Bali's spiritual landscape is adorned with a myriad of temples and sacred sites, each reflecting the island's rich religious heritage. From sea-facing temples to mountaintop shrines, these places of worship hold a sacred energy that resonates with both locals and visitors.

### Cultural and Spiritual Significance:
1. Balinese Hinduism: The predominant religion on the island is a unique blend of Hinduism and animism. Temples are central to the Balinese way of life, serving as places of devotion, community gatherings, and cultural expression.

2. Offerings and Rituals: The act of making daily offerings, or "canang sari," is a ubiquitous practice. Balinese believe that these offerings appease spirits and deities, fostering harmony and balance in the physical and spiritual realms.

**Exploring Bali's Temples:**
1. Besakih Temple: Often referred to as the "Mother Temple," Besakih is located on the slopes of Mount Agung and is the largest and holiest temple complex in Bali. It's a testament to Balinese devotion and boasts stunning mountain views.

2. Uluwatu Temple: Perched atop a dramatic cliff overlooking the Indian Ocean, Uluwatu Temple is renowned for its sunset Kecak dance performances and its commanding sea views.

3. Tanah Lot: An iconic temple perched on a rocky outcrop, Tanah Lot is best visited during sunset, when the temple's silhouette against the horizon creates a mesmerizing scene.

4. Tirta Empul: This sacred spring water temple near Ubud is known for its purification baths. Locals and visitors alike participate in the ritual bathing to cleanse their body and soul.

**Cultural Etiquette:**
1. Dress Modestly: When visiting temples, dress respectfully with shoulders and knees covered. Sarongs and sashes are often provided at the entrances if needed.

2. Silence and Respect: Observe the serene atmosphere and maintain silence during prayers or rituals. Respect the sacred space by refraining from climbing on shrines or walking in front of worshippers.

**Participating in Spiritual Rituals:**
1. Ceremonial Calendar: Bali's calendar is dotted with various temple festivals and ceremonies. If you're lucky to visit during such times, you'll witness vibrant processions, dance performances, and offerings.

2. Local Guides: Engage with local guides who can provide insights into temple architecture, symbolism, and the significance of rituals.

**Environmental and Cultural Preservation:**
As you explore these sacred sites, remember that they are living cultural heritage. Show appreciation by respecting the environment, refraining from disturbing offerings, and adhering to local customs.

Bali's temples and sacred sites offer an immersion into the island's spiritual heart, allowing you to connect with a culture steeped in reverence and tradition. As you traverse the lush landscapes and intricate architecture, you'll gain a deeper understanding of the island's soul. So, embrace the tranquility, marvel at the devotion, and let the spiritual energy of Bali's temples inspire you on your journey of cultural exploration.

### 7.1.1 *Besakih Temple*

Nestled on the slopes of the sacred Mount Agung, Besakih Temple is Bali's most revered and largest temple complex. Often referred to as the "Mother Temple," this ancient site holds deep spiritual significance and stands as a symbol of Balinese devotion and cultural heritage. In this comprehensive travel guide, we'll unravel the allure of Besakih Temple, exploring its history, architecture, religious significance, and practical tips for a meaningful visit.

Besakih Temple is a sprawling complex comprising 86 individual temples that span multiple levels on the southern slope of Mount Agung, Bali's highest peak. As the spiritual epicenter of the island,

Besakih is a place of worship, cultural ceremonies, and spiritual pilgrimage.

**Religious Significance:**
1. Balinese Hinduism: Besakih is the holiest of all temples in Bali and holds a special place in Balinese Hinduism. It's believed to be a place of connection between the gods and humans, embodying the concept of "Tri Hita Karana" - the harmonious balance between humans, nature, and the divine.

2. Mother Temple: The term "Mother Temple" refers to Besakih's status as the center of spiritual and religious activities in Bali. It influences the timing and rituals of other temples across the island.

**Temple Architecture:**
1. Tiers and Padas: The complex is organized into multiple terraced levels known as "padas." These levels are dedicated to different deities and are accessed via a grand staircase.

2. Meru Towers: The complex features numerous meru towers, distinctive pagoda-like structures with tiered roofs. Each meru is dedicated to a specific deity and signifies the connection between the human and divine realms.

**Exploring Besakih:**
1. Panorama Views: The higher you ascend within the complex, the more panoramic the views become. From the upper levels, you can gaze at the lush landscapes below and the towering presence of Mount Agung.

2. Ceremonies and Festivals: Besakih hosts several major festivals and ceremonies throughout the year, with the most significant being the "Eka Dasa Rudra," which occurs approximately once every century. During these events, the complex comes alive with vibrant processions, rituals, and performances.

**Practical Tips:**
1. Dress Code: Wear respectful attire covering shoulders and knees. Sarongs and sashes can be rented at the entrance if needed.

2. Guides: Engage a local guide to provide insights into the temple's history, rituals, and architectural details. This enriches your understanding of the complex.

3. Cultural Etiquette: Show reverence by maintaining silence during prayers, not stepping on

offerings, and following any instructions given by temple staff.

**Environmental and Cultural Preservation:**
As a visitor, you play a role in preserving the sanctity of Besakih. Refrain from touching religious objects, entering restricted areas, or interfering with ongoing ceremonies.

Besakih Temple is a testament to Bali's deep spiritual roots and rich cultural heritage. As you ascend its terraced levels, you'll feel a profound sense of connection to the island's essence. The architectural grandeur, the panoramic vistas, and the energy of devotion combine to create an experience that transcends the physical realm. So, embrace the spiritual aura, admire the architectural marvels, and let the energy of Besakih Temple envelop you in a journey of the soul that will linger long after you've left its sacred grounds.

### 7.1.2 *Uluwatu Temple*

Perched dramatically on the edge of a sheer cliff overlooking the Indian Ocean, Uluwatu Temple is a Bali icon that captivates visitors with its breathtaking views, traditional performances, and spiritual significance. With a backdrop of crashing waves and a sense of ancient mystique, Uluwatu

Temple offers a unique blend of natural beauty, cultural experiences, and historical significance. In this comprehensive travel guide, we'll uncover the allure of Uluwatu Temple, exploring its history, architecture, Kecak dance performances, and practical tips for an unforgettable visit.

Uluwatu Temple, also known as Pura Luhur Uluwatu, is located on the southwestern tip of Bali's Bukit Peninsula. Its cliffside location, perched 70 meters above the Indian Ocean, makes it one of the most scenic and revered temples on the island.

**Religious Significance:**
1. Balinese Hinduism: Uluwatu Temple holds deep spiritual importance in Balinese Hinduism. It is dedicated to Sang Hyang Widhi Wasa (the Supreme God) and is one of Bali's nine key directional temples that are believed to protect the island from evil spirits.

2. Purity and Awe: The temple's location is believed to harness the spiritual energy of the ocean and the winds, infusing the temple with a sense of purity and awe-inspiring power.

**Temple Architecture:**

1. Cliffside Architecture: Uluwatu Temple's unique architecture harmonizes with the natural landscape. The gateways and shrines are adorned with intricate stone carvings, showcasing the artistic prowess of Balinese artisans.

2. Sea Facing: The temple's orientation towards the sea enhances its mystical atmosphere, creating an ideal spot to witness the sunset over the Indian Ocean.

**Kecak Dance Performances:**
1. Sunset Spectacle: Uluwatu Temple is renowned for its sunset Kecak dance performances. Against the backdrop of the setting sun, the Kecak dancers enact scenes from the Ramayana epic, accompanied by rhythmic chants and the mesmerizing sounds of the gamelan.

2. Cultural Expression: The Kecak dance is not only a form of entertainment but also a cultural expression that showcases Bali's traditional storytelling through dance and music.

**Practical Tips:**
1. Sun Protection: As Uluwatu Temple is perched on a cliff, bring sun protection such as a hat,

sunglasses, and sunscreen to shield yourself from the strong sun.

2. Dress Code: Wear respectful attire covering shoulders and knees. Sarongs and sashes are provided at the entrance if needed.

3. Monkey Interactions: The temple is also home to a population of monkeys. While they can be entertaining, exercise caution and avoid feeding or provoking them.

**Environmental and Cultural Respect:**
To preserve the temple's sanctity and minimize environmental impact, visitors should avoid touching sacred objects, refrain from littering, and respect the silence during prayers and performances.

Uluwatu Temple is a harmonious blend of Bali's natural beauty, spiritual devotion, and cultural richness. As you stand on the cliff, gazing at the horizon and witnessing the dance of light and waves, you'll feel the mystical energy that permeates this sacred place. The Kecak dance performance adds a vibrant cultural dimension to your visit, enriching your understanding of Bali's artistic heritage. Uluwatu Temple invites you to connect with Bali's essence, to be swept away by its beauty, and to experience a unique encounter between humanity and the divine against the backdrop of the endless ocean.

### *7.1.3 Tirta Empul Temple*

Discover the serene oasis of Tirta Empul Temple, a place where ancient rituals, pristine waters, and spiritual devotion converge. Nestled near the town of Tampaksiring in Bali, this enchanting water temple holds profound significance for both locals and visitors seeking a soul-cleansing experience. In this comprehensive travel guide, we'll delve into the allure of Tirta Empul Temple, exploring its history, rituals, unique purification pools, and practical tips for a meaningful visit.

Tirta Empul Temple, also known as "Holy Spring Water Temple," is a revered Hindu temple complex located in the lush surroundings of central Bali. The temple is known for its sacred springs that are believed to have powerful cleansing and healing properties.

**Spiritual Significance:**
1. Balinese Hindu Rituals: Tirta Empul Temple is renowned for its purification rituals. Balinese Hindus believe that bathing in the holy spring

waters can cleanse the soul, heal the body, and protect against negative influences.

2. Mythological Origins: Legend has it that the temple's sacred springs were created by the god Indra, who pierced the earth to provide healing waters for his troops.

**Temple Architecture:**
1. Architectural Harmony: Tirta Empul's architecture reflects Bali's unique style. The complex features traditional Balinese design elements, stone carvings, and pavilions.

2. Main Courtyard: The central courtyard houses the purification pools. A series of fountains and spouts release the spring water, which devotees use for ceremonial cleansing.

**Ritual Bathing and Purification:**
1. Holy Springs: The temple has a main bathing area with several pools fed by the holy springs. Devotees and visitors immerse themselves in the pools, following specific rituals of purification and offering prayers.

2. Pilgrimage Destination: Tirta Empul is a popular pilgrimage site during significant Balinese Hindu

festivals. Witnessing the rituals and participating in the ceremonies offers a unique cultural experience.

**Practical Tips:**
1. Dress Modestly: Wear respectful attire covering shoulders and knees. Sarongs and sashes can be rented at the entrance if needed.

2. Guidance: Engage a local guide to provide insights into the temple's history, rituals, and cultural significance. They can also guide you through the purification process.

3. Participation: If you wish to participate in the purification ritual, observe and follow the actions of the locals. They can guide you on how to respectfully join in.

**Cultural and Environmental Respect:**
During your visit, uphold the sanctity of Tirta Empul Temple by maintaining a respectful demeanor, avoiding loud conversations, and refraining from littering.

Tirta Empul Temple offers a transformative experience that transcends the physical realm. As you step into the pristine waters, you'll connect with centuries of devotion, spiritual beliefs, and the island's sacred heritage. The temple's tranquil surroundings and the ethereal sound of flowing water create an atmosphere that invites inner reflection and rejuvenation. Tirta Empul Temple is a place where ancient rituals and contemporary reverence intersect, offering a profound encounter with Bali's spiritual essence. So, step into the cleansing waters, embrace the sacred energy, and emerge with a renewed sense of balance and serenity that will linger in your heart long after you've left the temple's hallowed grounds.

## 7.2 Traditional Balinese Dance Performances

Journey into the heart of Bali's artistic heritage through the captivating world of traditional Balinese dance performances. Infused with intricate movements, vibrant costumes, and rich cultural narratives, these performances offer travelers an immersive glimpse into the island's soul. In this comprehensive travel guide, we'll explore the enchantment of traditional Balinese dance, from its origins and diverse forms to the significance of various performances and practical tips for experiencing these cultural treasures.

Traditional Balinese dance is more than just a series of movements; it's a storytelling medium that has been passed down through generations. These performances not only showcase the island's artistic prowess but also serve as a window into the Balinese way of life and belief system.

**Origins and Forms:**
1. Rooted in Mythology: Many Balinese dances are inspired by Hindu epics, mythological tales, and local folklore. Each performance tells a story, often involving gods, demons, and heroes.

2. Rich Variety: Balinese dance encompasses a diverse range of forms, each with its own unique characteristics, costumes, and music. Some well-known forms include Legong, Barong, Kecak, and Pendet.

**Significance and Symbolism:**
1. Spiritual Expression: Dance is a spiritual offering to the gods and ancestors. Performers often prepare themselves through rituals and meditation before taking the stage.

2. Balinese Philosophy: The dances reflect Balinese philosophy, emphasizing harmony, balance, and the concept of "Tri Hita Karana" - the interconnectedness between humans, nature, and the divine.

**Popular Dance Performances:**
1. Legong Dance: Graceful and delicate, Legong dance involves intricate hand and eye movements. It often tells stories of love and mythical beings.

2. Barong Dance: The Barong represents good and the Rangda symbolizes evil. This dance is a battle between these forces, exploring the constant struggle between light and darkness.

3. Kecak Dance: The Kecak dance is known for its hypnotic chanting and synchronized rhythmic movements. It often depicts scenes from the Ramayana epic.

**Experiencing Balinese Dance:**
1. Venue Selection: Traditional Balinese dance performances are held in various venues across the island, from temples to cultural centers and tourist areas.

2. Engage with Locals: Interact with locals to gain insights into the stories behind the performances, the significance of the costumes, and the cultural context of the dances.

**Practical Tips:**

1. Attire: Dress modestly and wear sarongs and sashes if required, as a sign of respect for the sacred nature of the performances.

2. Seating: Arrive early to secure a good seat. Some performances are held in open-air amphitheaters, adding to the immersive experience.

3. Photography: While photography is often permitted, avoid using flash and be mindful of not disturbing performers or other audience members.

**Cultural Respect:**
Show appreciation for the cultural significance of these performances by maintaining silence during the show, refraining from talking, and turning off your phone.

Traditional Balinese dance performances are a window into the island's artistic soul, offering a profound connection to its history, beliefs, and cultural heritage. As you watch the dancers gracefully move and hear the melodies that accompany them, you'll feel the energy and dedication that goes into each performance. Embrace the enchantment, immerse yourself in the stories, and let the rhythm of the dance transport you into a world where tradition and artistry intertwine, leaving an indelible mark on your Bali journey.

### 7.3 Art Markets and Handicrafts

Indulge your senses and immerse yourself in the vibrant world of Balinese art and craftsmanship through the island's bustling art markets and unique handicrafts. From intricate wood carvings to intricate textiles and traditional paintings, Bali's art scene is a kaleidoscope of colors, textures, and cultural expression. In this comprehensive travel guide, we'll dive into the realm of art markets and handicrafts, exploring their significance, diverse offerings, and practical tips for an enriching shopping experience.

Bali's art markets and handicrafts are an integral part of the island's cultural fabric. These markets not only offer an opportunity to acquire one-of-a-kind souvenirs but also provide insight into the island's artistic heritage and craftsmanship.

**Artistic Significance:**
1. Cultural Expression: Balinese art is deeply rooted in spirituality, tradition, and mythology. Handicrafts are a form of cultural expression that reflects the Balinese way of life, beliefs, and aesthetics.

2. Craftsmanship: The creation of handicrafts often involves intricate techniques passed down through generations. Each piece is a testament to the artisans' skill and dedication.

**Exploring Art Markets:**
1. Ubud Market: Located in the heart of Ubud, this market is renowned for its eclectic array of arts and crafts, from textiles and jewelry to wood carvings and paintings.

2. Sukawati Art Market: This market specializes in traditional Balinese arts and crafts, offering a wide range of items at affordable prices.

3. Sanur Art Market: Sanur's market is a treasure trove of local crafts, including woven baskets, sarongs, and batik fabrics.

**Diverse Handicrafts:**
1. Wood Carvings: Bali is celebrated for its intricate wood carvings that range from exquisite statues of deities and animals to ornate doors and furniture.

2. Textiles: Batik, ikat, and songket are traditional Balinese textiles characterized by intricate designs and vibrant colors.

3. Paintings: Balinese paintings often depict mythological scenes, nature, and daily life. They come in various styles, including traditional and contemporary.

**Practical Tips:**
1. Quality Assessment: When purchasing handicrafts, examine the quality of materials, intricate details, and finish to ensure you're getting an authentic piece.

2. Bargaining: Bargaining is a common practice in Bali's markets. Approach it with respect and a friendly attitude, keeping in mind that artisans' work deserves fair compensation.

3. Cultural Sensitivity: Be mindful when photographing vendors and their goods. Always ask for permission and respect their wishes.

**Supporting Local Artisans:**
By purchasing handicrafts directly from local markets, you're supporting the livelihoods of Balinese artisans and contributing to the preservation of traditional craftsmanship.

**Environmental and Ethical Considerations:**

Choose items made from sustainable materials and support businesses that prioritize ethical production practices and fair wages for artisans.

Exploring Bali's art markets and handicrafts is a journey into the heart of the island's cultural heritage. As you peruse the stalls, you'll discover the intricate artistry, devotion, and craftsmanship that go into each piece. From the richly colored textiles to the ornate wood carvings, each item tells a story of tradition, creativity, and the island's vibrant soul. So, wander through the bustling markets, engage with local artisans, and leave with more than just souvenirs – take with you the essence of Bali's artistic spirit, which will continue to inspire you long after your journey ends.

### 7.4 Balinese Cooking Classes

Embark on a delectable journey through the flavors of Bali by participating in Balinese cooking classes. Delve into the island's rich culinary traditions, aromatic spices, and vibrant ingredients as you learn to craft traditional dishes under the guidance of local chefs. In this comprehensive travel guide, we'll explore the allure of Balinese cooking classes, from their cultural significance and immersive experiences to the practical tips for creating your own authentic Balinese feast.

Balinese cooking classes offer a unique opportunity to not only savor the island's exquisite cuisine but also to dive into the heart of its culture and lifestyle. These classes provide a hands-on experience that immerses you in the art of Balinese cooking, revealing the secrets of traditional recipes passed down through generations.

**Cultural Significance:**
1. Heritage Preservation: Balinese cooking is a fundamental aspect of the island's culture, reflecting its Hindu beliefs, indigenous ingredients, and culinary customs.

2. Community and Sharing: Cooking is a communal activity in Bali, often involving family members coming together to prepare meals and share stories.

Immersive Experience:
1. Local Markets: Many cooking classes start with a visit to local markets, where you'll learn about Balinese ingredients and select fresh produce.

2. Hands-On Cooking: Under the guidance of skilled chefs, you'll learn to prepare a range of Balinese dishes, from savory curries to fragrant rice dishes.

3. Traditional Techniques: Balinese cooking classes often introduce you to traditional methods of grinding spices, making sauces, and cooking over open flames.

**Popular Balinese Dishes:**
1. Nasi Goreng: Balinese fried rice cooked with a blend of aromatic spices, vegetables, and often served with a fried egg on top.

2. Babi Guling: Spit-roasted, succulent pig stuffed with a mix of spices, herbs, and vegetables, making it a centerpiece of festive occasions.

3. Lawar: A traditional dish made with minced meat (usually pork or chicken), vegetables, and spices, often served with rice.

**Practical Tips:**
1. Booking: Reserve your cooking class in advance through reputable operators or your accommodation.

2. Attire: Wear comfortable clothing and consider bringing an apron, as hands-on cooking can get a bit messy.

3. Allergies and Preferences: Inform the instructor about any dietary restrictions, allergies, or preferences before the class begins.

**Culinary Etiquette:**
Show appreciation for Balinese culinary traditions by actively participating, showing respect for the instructors, and savoring each dish you create.

**Environmental Considerations:**
Choose cooking classes that prioritize sustainability by using locally sourced ingredients and promoting eco-friendly practices.

Participating in Balinese cooking classes is an invitation to connect with the heart of Bali's culture through the universal language of food. As you chop, stir, and savor the ingredients, you'll not only master the art of Balinese cuisine but also gain insight into the island's traditions, beliefs, and way of life. Balinese cooking classes are a memory-making experience, a delightful culinary adventure that will continue to inspire your palate long after you've returned home. So, roll up your sleeves, embrace the aromas, and let the flavors of Bali guide you on a journey of taste, culture, and connection.

# CHAPTER 8: Indulging in Balinese Cuisine

## 8.1 Must-Try Dishes and Local Delicacies

Embark on a culinary adventure through the vibrant tapestry of Balinese cuisine, where aromatic spices, fresh ingredients, and cultural heritage converge to create a symphony of flavors. From fiery curries to sweet desserts, Bali's culinary landscape offers a myriad of dishes that tantalize the taste buds and provide insight into the island's rich culture. In this comprehensive travel guide, we'll delve into the world of must-try Balinese dishes and local delicacies, from their historical roots to practical tips for sampling these delectable treats.

Balinese cuisine is a reflection of the island's history, geography, and deep-rooted traditions. Influenced by indigenous ingredients and a blend of culinary cultures, the island's dishes celebrate the balance of flavors and the artistry of cooking.

Nasi Campur: A quintessential Balinese meal, "nasi campur" is a plate of mixed dishes featuring rice as the centerpiece. It includes a variety of side dishes, such as vegetables, meats, and sauces.

Babi Guling: A festive dish reserved for special occasions, "babi guling" is a spit-roasted suckling pig marinated with a blend of spices, herbs, and turmeric. The result is succulent meat with crispy skin.

Ayam Betutu: This dish consists of chicken marinated with traditional spices, wrapped in banana leaves, and slow-cooked until tender. The aromatic spices infuse the meat with rich flavors.

Bebek Betutu: Similar to Ayam Betutu, this dish features duck marinated with a blend of spices, wrapped, and slow-cooked to perfection.

Lawar: A traditional mix containing finely chopped meat (often pork), vegetables, and grated coconut mixed with rich herbs and spices.

Sate Lilit: Balinese satay made from minced fish, chicken, pork, or beef. The meat is mixed with grated coconut, coconut milk, lime leaves, and a blend of spices before being threaded onto skewers and grilled.

Rendang: Although originating from neighboring Indonesia, Balinese rendang is a slow-cooked meat dish that features tender beef in a rich, fragrant coconut curry.

Bebek Betutu: This dish features duck marinated with a blend of spices, wrapped in banana leaves, and slow-cooked to tender perfection.

**Local Delicacies and Desserts:**
Jaja Bali: A colorful assortment of traditional Balinese sweets, often made from glutinous rice flour and coconut.

Dadar Gulung: Also known as "green pancake," this dessert features pandan-flavored crepes rolled with sweet coconut and palm sugar filling.

Klepon: Green rice cakes filled with palm sugar and coated in grated coconut. They offer a delightful blend of textures and flavors.

**Practical Tips:**
1. Exploring Warungs: Local eateries known as "warungs" offer an authentic taste of Balinese cuisine. Don't hesitate to ask for recommendations from locals or fellow travelers.

2. Market Experiences: Visit local markets to experience fresh ingredients, discover lesser-known

dishes, and immerse yourself in the island's culinary culture.

3. Food Tours: Join guided food tours to navigate the diverse range of Balinese dishes, learn about their history, and indulge in expertly curated meals.

**Cultural Etiquette:**
When dining in local settings, use your right hand for eating, as the left hand is considered impolite. Show appreciation for the meal by leaving a small amount of food on your plate after eating.

**Environmental and Ethical Considerations:**
Opt for establishments that prioritize locally sourced, sustainable ingredients, and contribute to the well-being of the community.

Exploring Bali's culinary landscape is an adventure that engages all your senses. From the spicy aromas of curries to the vibrant colors of sweet desserts, each dish reflects the island's cultural identity. As you indulge in the flavors, you're not just tasting food; you're experiencing a piece of Bali's history, heritage, and heart. So, savor each bite, embrace the bold spices, and let the variety of flavors guide you on a gastronomic journey that leaves an indelible mark on your Bali memories.

## 8.2 Popular Warungs and Restaurants

Embark on a culinary journey through Bali's diverse dining scene, where traditional warungs and contemporary restaurants offer a tantalizing array of flavors that cater to every palate. From humble street-side eateries to upscale dining establishments, Bali's food culture showcases the island's rich culinary heritage and global influences. In this comprehensive travel guide, we'll explore some of Bali's popular warungs and restaurants, from their distinctive offerings and ambiances to practical tips for savoring the best of Bali's culinary delights.

Bali's dining scene is a tapestry of traditional flavors, international cuisines, and innovative creations. Whether you're seeking an authentic Balinese feast or indulging in gourmet delights, the island's warungs and restaurants offer a diverse range of options to satisfy your cravings.

**Popular Warungs:**
1. Warung Babi Guling Ibu Oka (Ubud): Renowned for its succulent roast pork, this warung serves up the celebrated Balinese dish, "babi guling," accompanied by flavorful side dishes.

2. Warung Sopa (Ubud): A vegetarian-friendly warung that offers a diverse selection of plant-based dishes, showcasing the abundance of locally sourced ingredients.

3. Warung Made (Seminyak): A long-standing establishment known for its authentic Balinese dishes and vibrant atmosphere, offering everything from nasi campur to satay.

**Contemporary Restaurants:**
1. Locavore (Ubud): A fine-dining establishment that celebrates local ingredients and culinary craftsmanship, offering a tasting menu that fuses Balinese and international flavors.

2. Mozaic (Ubud): Known for its artistic presentation and innovative cuisine, Mozaic offers an intimate dining experience that combines French cooking techniques with Balinese ingredients.

3. Merah Putih (Seminyak): A stylish restaurant that reinterprets Indonesian cuisine, featuring a menu that showcases regional dishes prepared with a modern twist.

**Beachfront Dining:**

1. La Lucciola (Seminyak): Nestled along Seminyak Beach, this restaurant offers Italian-inspired cuisine with stunning ocean views, making it a popular spot for both dining and sunset cocktails.

2. Sundays Beach Club (Uluwatu): A unique dining experience right on the beach, Sundays offers a relaxed atmosphere and a menu featuring a mix of international and Indonesian dishes.

**Practical Tips:**
1. Reservations: For popular restaurants, it's advisable to make reservations, especially during peak tourist seasons.

2. Dress Code: While most warungs have a casual dress code, upscale restaurants may have specific dress requirements, so it's best to check in advance.

3. Opening Hours: Be mindful of opening hours, as some places may close on certain days of the week or have limited lunch or dinner hours.

**Environmental and Ethical Considerations:**
Opt for eateries that emphasize sustainability, locally sourced ingredients, and eco-friendly practices, contributing to the well-being of the community and the environment.

Bali's dining scene is a gastronomic adventure that encapsulates the island's diversity, creativity, and culinary excellence. From savoring Balinese specialties at a local warung to indulging in innovative creations at upscale restaurants, each dining experience unveils a different facet of Bali's cultural mosaic. As you immerse yourself in the flavors and ambiances of Bali's dining establishments, you're not just satisfying your appetite – you're embarking on a culinary journey that enriches your understanding of the island's soul and leaves an indelible mark on your travel memories.

### *8.3 Vegan and Vegetarian Options*

Embrace Bali's flourishing vegan and vegetarian culinary scene, where fresh ingredients, creative recipes, and cultural diversity come together to offer a delightful array of plant-based options. From colorful salads to innovative meat-free creations, the island's eateries cater to health-conscious travelers and those seeking ethical dining choices. In this comprehensive travel guide, we'll explore Bali's vegan and vegetarian offerings, from their diversity and popularity to practical tips for enjoying Bali's plant-based cuisine to the fullest.

Bali's embrace of vegan and vegetarian cuisine is a reflection of the island's health-conscious mindset, cultural openness, and commitment to sustainable living. Whether you're an ardent vegan, a curious foodie, or simply seeking a fresh and nourishing meal, Bali's vegan and vegetarian scene has something for everyone.

**Diverse Offerings:**
1. Vegan Warungs: Traditional Balinese warungs are embracing vegan and vegetarian options, offering local dishes that have been reimagined with plant-based ingredients.

2. Plant-Based Cafes: Bali is home to a growing number of cafes dedicated exclusively to vegan and vegetarian cuisine. These cafes often feature creative dishes that cater to diverse dietary preferences.

3. Raw Food Delights: Experience the raw food movement in Bali with cafes that specialize in uncooked, plant-based cuisine, from zucchini noodles to raw desserts.

**Popularity and Acceptance:**

1. Ubiquitous Choices: Vegan and vegetarian options are readily available across Bali, from busy tourist areas to more off-the-beaten-path locations.

2. Cultural Adaptation: Balinese cuisine is known for its diverse ingredients, making it relatively easy to adapt dishes to plant-based versions.

**Iconic Vegan and Vegetarian Dishes:**
1. Nasi Campur Vegan: A vegan twist on the traditional nasi campur, this dish offers an array of plant-based side dishes served with rice.

2. Jackfruit Rendang: Jackfruit is used as a meat substitute in this vegan rendition of the traditional Indonesian dish, "rendang."

3. Gado-Gado: A popular Indonesian salad featuring steamed vegetables, tofu, tempeh, and peanut sauce, often available in vegan versions.

**Practical Tips:**
1. Research and Reviews: Utilize online resources and reviews to find vegan and vegetarian-friendly eateries in your chosen location.

2. Customization: Don't hesitate to ask for vegan or vegetarian versions of menu items at non-vegan

restaurants. Many places are accommodating and willing to adapt.

3. Language Barriers: Carry a small card or use translation apps to communicate your dietary preferences and restrictions in Indonesian.

**Ethical and Environmental Considerations:**
By choosing vegan and vegetarian options, you're contributing to a more sustainable and ethical dining culture that supports plant-based ingredients and reduces the carbon footprint.

Bali's vegan and vegetarian scene invites you to explore the intersection of flavor, wellness, and sustainability. From savoring traditional Balinese dishes to embracing innovative plant-based creations, each meal is an opportunity to nourish your body while respecting the environment and local cultures. As you embark on your culinary exploration of Bali's vegan and vegetarian offerings, you're not just dining – you're contributing to a movement that embraces conscious consumption and celebrates the harmony between food, health, and the planet.

# CHAPTER 9: Practical Tips for a Smooth Trip

## *9.1 Accommodation Options*

Bali's enchanting landscapes and vibrant culture are complemented by a diverse range of accommodation options that cater to every traveler's desires and preferences. From luxurious resorts to charming guesthouses, each lodging choice provides a unique backdrop to your Bali adventure. In this comprehensive travel guide, we'll explore a variety of accommodation options in Bali, offering insights into their features, ambiance, and notable examples to help you make an informed choice for your stay.

**Luxury Resorts and Villas:**
1. Features: Opulent accommodations often include private pool villas, exquisite design, spa facilities, and personalized service.

2. Ambiance: Ideal for travelers seeking exclusivity, privacy, and pampering amid stunning surroundings.

3. Notable Examples: AYANA Resort and Spa, The Mulia, The Royal Purnama, Alila Villas Uluwatu.

**Beachfront Escapes:**
1. Features: Direct access to pristine beaches, sea-view rooms, water sports facilities, and beachfront dining.

2. Ambiance: Perfect for beach enthusiasts, honeymooners, and those who cherish breathtaking ocean views.

3. Notable Examples: The Legian Bali, Samabe Bali Suites & Villas, Karma Kandara, Grand Mirage Resort & Thalasso Bali.

**Ubud Retreats:**
1. Features: Nestled in the lush surroundings of Ubud, often with traditional Balinese architecture, yoga studios, and cultural activities.

2. Ambiance: Ideal for seekers of serenity, culture, and artistic inspiration.

3. Notable Examples: Fivelements Retreat Bali, COMO Uma Ubud, Kamandalu Ubud, Bisma Eight.

**Eco-Friendly Stays:**
1. Features: Sustainable practices, eco-conscious design, organic gardens, and eco-friendly amenities.

2. Ambiance: Suited for eco-conscious travelers who want to minimize their environmental footprint.

3. Notable Examples: Green Village Bali, Bambu Indah, Sarinbuana Eco Lodge, Potato Head Studios.

**Traditional Accommodations:**
1. Features: Cultural immersion, personalized service, authentic Balinese decor, and warm hospitality.

2. Ambiance: Perfect for travelers seeking an authentic experience and a deeper connection with Balinese traditions.

3. Notable Examples: Puri Gangga Resort, Puri Sunia Resort, Pondok Sebatu Villa, Taman Bebek Bali.

**Budget-Friendly Options:**
1. Features: Basic amenities, affordable rates, communal spaces, and opportunities for social interaction.

2. Ambiance: Suited for budget-conscious travelers, backpackers, and those seeking a laid-back atmosphere.

3. Notable Examples: The Farm Hostel, Pudak Sari Unizou Hostel, Capsule Hostel Bali, M Box Seminyak.

**Practical Tips:**
1. Location Consideration: Choose accommodations that align with your planned activities and preferences.
2. Reviews and Recommendations: Utilize online reviews and recommendations to ensure the quality and suitability of your chosen accommodation.
3. Direct Booking: Contact accommodations directly to inquire about availability, amenities, and any special offers.

As you embark on your Bali journey, your chosen accommodation becomes your sanctuary and a part of your travel narrative. Each lodging option offers a unique lens through which to experience the island's beauty, culture, and warmth. From luxury resorts to eco-friendly stays, embrace the opportunity to create cherished memories in the heart of Bali's diverse landscapes, leaving you with a sense of fulfillment and connection long after your adventure comes to an end.

## 9.2 Getting Around: Transportation Guide

Bali, a stunning tropical paradise known for its lush landscapes, pristine beaches, and rich cultural heritage, is a popular travel destination that attracts millions of visitors each year. Navigating this Indonesian island can be an exciting adventure, but it's essential to have a solid understanding of the transportation options available to make the most of your trip. From bustling streets to tranquil countryside, Bali offers various modes of transportation that cater to different preferences and budgets. This comprehensive transportation guide will delve into the intricacies of getting around in Bali, providing you with insights and tips to ensure a smooth and enjoyable travel experience.

### Modes of Transportation

**Scooters and Motorbikes**
Scooters and motorbikes are ubiquitous on the roads of Bali, offering a flexible and convenient way to explore the island. They provide a sense of freedom, allowing travelers to navigate narrow streets, beat traffic, and discover hidden gems.

However, renting a scooter requires a valid international driver's license and a careful understanding of local traffic rules. It's essential to wear a helmet and exercise caution while driving, as road conditions can vary.

**Taxis and Ride-Sharing Services**
Taxis are prevalent in Bali, and you'll find them at airports, tourist areas, and major towns. Blue Bird taxis are known for their reliability and use of meters. Additionally, ride-sharing services like Grab have gained popularity, offering a more convenient and often cheaper alternative to traditional taxis. These services provide a fixed price before the ride, reducing the chances of haggling or overcharging.

**Private Drivers**
Hiring a private driver is an excellent option for those seeking a more personalized experience. Drivers often double as guides, offering local insights and recommendations. You can negotiate the itinerary, allowing you to visit both popular attractions and off-the-beaten-path sites. This mode of transportation is ideal for families or groups looking for a comfortable and hassle-free way to explore Bali.

**Public Buses**

Public buses are a cost-effective means of transportation in Bali. While they may not be as frequent or punctual as other options, they provide a unique opportunity to interact with locals and experience daily life on the island. Bemos, small vans converted into public transport, are a common sight and offer routes within towns and between major destinations.

Navigating Bali's Roads

**Traffic and Road Conditions**
Bali's roads can be a mix of well-paved highways, narrow streets, and bumpy roads through rural areas. Traffic congestion is a common occurrence, especially in tourist-heavy areas like Kuta and Seminyak. During peak hours, it's advisable to plan your travels accordingly and allow extra time for potential delays.

**Navigational Challenges**
While Bali's road network has improved over the years, navigating can still be challenging due to the lack of consistent street signs. GPS navigation apps can be a lifesaver, helping you find your way around

without getting lost. However, keep in mind that some remote areas might not have accurate digital maps, so it's wise to have a physical map as a backup.

## Safety Considerations

### Driving Etiquette
If you're considering renting a scooter or motorbike, remember that driving etiquette and rules in Bali may differ from what you're accustomed to. Always drive defensively, anticipate the behavior of other road users, and be cautious at intersections. Remember to use your horn as a polite signal, rather than an aggressive one.

### Wearing Helmets and Protective Gear
Wearing helmets and appropriate protective gear is not just a legal requirement but also a crucial safety measure. Bali's roads can be unpredictable, and accidents can happen. Prioritize your safety by ensuring that you and any passengers are properly equipped before setting off on your journey.

### Travel Insurance
Before embarking on your Bali adventure, make sure you have comprehensive travel insurance that

covers medical emergencies, accidents, and potential damages to rental vehicles. This will provide you with peace of mind in case unforeseen events occur during your travels.

## Getting to and From the Airport

### Ngurah Rai International Airport
Bali's main airport, Ngurah Rai International Airport, is located in Denpasar. Upon arrival, you'll find various transportation options to take you to your accommodation. Taxis, ride-sharing services, and pre-arranged transfers are readily available. Blue Bird taxis have a reliable presence at the airport, ensuring a safe and metered ride to your destination.

## Exploring Beyond the Tourist Hubs

### Rural Areas and Countryside
To truly experience Bali's authentic charm, consider venturing beyond the well-trodden tourist hubs. In rural areas and the countryside, transportation options might be limited, and some destinations might only be accessible by motorbike or private vehicle. Embrace the adventure and take advantage

of the opportunity to immerse yourself in local culture.

## Environmental Considerations

**Sustainable Transportation Choices**
As responsible travelers, it's essential to consider the environmental impact of our transportation choices. Opt for eco-friendly modes of transportation when possible, such as walking or cycling for short distances. Additionally, some hotels and resorts offer bicycle rentals as part of their amenities, allowing you to explore nearby areas while minimizing your carbon footprint.

Navigating Bali's diverse landscapes and vibrant culture is an enriching experience that involves careful consideration of transportation options. Whether you're seeking the thrill of driving a scooter through bustling streets or the comfort of a private driver guiding you through hidden gems, Bali offers a range of transportation choices to suit different preferences. By prioritizing safety, respecting local customs, and making sustainable choices, you can embark on a memorable journey that captures the essence of this enchanting island.

## 9.3 Language Basics

Bali, with its rich cultural heritage and diverse communities, offers a unique blend of languages that reflect its vibrant history. While Bahasa Indonesia is the official language of Indonesia, including Bali, the island also boasts local dialects, traditional languages, and an array of foreign tongues spoken due to its popularity as a tourist destination. Navigating these linguistic nuances can greatly enhance your travel experience, allowing you to connect more deeply with the local culture and people. In this comprehensive guide, we'll delve into the language basics of Bali, offering insights and practical tips for effective communication during your stay.

### Bahasa Indonesia: The National Language

Bahasa Indonesia is the official language of Bali and the entire country. While English is commonly spoken in tourist areas, having a few basic phrases in Bahasa Indonesia can go a long way in establishing rapport with locals and immersing yourself in the local culture. Greetings, polite phrases, and common expressions are essential for smooth interactions.

## Common Phrases in Bahasa Indonesia

- Selamat pagi: Good morning
- Selamat siang: Good afternoon
- Selamat malam: Good evening
- Terima kasih: Thank you
- Tolong: Please
- Maaf: Excuse me/sorry
- Saya tidak mengerti: I don't understand
- Berapa harganya?: How much does it cost?
- Di mana...?: Where is...?

## Local Dialects and Languages

### Balinese Language
The Balinese people have their own language, Balinese, which is distinct from Bahasa Indonesia. While many Balinese people are bilingual and can converse in both languages, understanding a few Balinese words or phrases can help you connect on a more personal level. The Balinese language is rich in cultural significance and is often used in traditional ceremonies and performances.

### English: A Bridge to Communication

### English in Bali
English is widely spoken in tourist areas, hotels, restaurants, and shops. While the level of proficiency can vary, especially in more remote areas, you'll generally find that many people can communicate effectively in English. However, making an effort to use local phrases can be appreciated by locals and can create a more authentic experience.

## Non-Verbal Communication

### Respectful Gestures
Non-verbal communication plays a significant role in Bali, where gestures and body language are integral to conveying respect and politeness. For example, it's customary to offer and receive items, like money or souvenirs, with your right hand. The left hand is considered impolite for such interactions.

### Balinese Hand Gestures (Mudras)
In addition to common gestures, Balinese culture features intricate hand gestures known as mudras. These gestures are an essential part of traditional dance, drama, and religious ceremonies. While mastering these mudras might be challenging,

recognizing their significance can deepen your understanding of local performances and rituals.

## Cultural Sensitivity and Language

### Polite Address and Titles
Addressing people with the appropriate titles and terms of respect is vital in Balinese culture. Using "Pak" for men and "Ibu" for women followed by their first name shows politeness. If you're unsure, using "Bapak" for Mr. and "Ibu" for Mrs. is a safe choice.

## Language Learning Resources

### Language Apps and Books
To enhance your language skills before or during your trip, consider using language learning apps or phrasebooks. Apps like Duolingo or Memrise offer Bahasa Indonesia courses, allowing you to practice on the go. Phrasebooks can be handy for quick reference when you're out exploring.

Mastering the language basics in Bali not only facilitates practical communication but also fosters deeper connections with the local community.

Whether you're engaging in everyday interactions, navigating local markets, or participating in traditional ceremonies, a few well-chosen words can bridge cultural gaps and enrich your travel experience. By embracing the linguistic diversity of Bali, you'll open doors to meaningful interactions and a greater appreciation for the island's heritage.

## 9.4 Internet and Communication

In the digital age, staying connected while traveling has become essential for both convenience and safety. Bali, with its breathtaking landscapes and vibrant culture, is no exception. Whether you need to share your adventures on social media, keep in touch with loved ones, or access essential information, understanding the internet and communication options available on the island is crucial. In this comprehensive guide, we'll explore the intricacies of internet connectivity, mobile networks, communication apps, and other essentials to ensure you remain connected throughout your Bali journey.

### Internet Connectivity in Bali

**Availability of Internet**

Bali's urban and tourist areas generally offer reliable internet connectivity, but the quality can vary. Major towns like Kuta, Seminyak, and Ubud tend to have better internet access compared to more remote or rural areas. Many hotels, cafes, and restaurants offer free Wi-Fi, making it convenient to stay online while enjoying your meals or downtime.

**Mobile Data and SIM Cards**

Purchasing a local SIM card is a popular option for travelers who want continuous internet access. Upon arrival at Ngurah Rai International Airport, you'll find kiosks offering SIM cards with varying data plans. Providers like Telkomsel, XL Axiata, and Indosat offer packages that include data, calls, and texts. Make sure your phone is unlocked to use a local SIM card.

Mobile Networks and Coverage

**Telkomsel**

Telkomsel is one of Indonesia's leading mobile network providers and offers extensive coverage across Bali. Their "SimPATI" SIM cards are widely available and come with various data packages to suit different needs. Telkomsel's coverage is generally reliable, even in some rural areas.

### XL Axiata
XL Axiata is another popular choice, offering competitive data packages for tourists. Their "XPLOR" SIM cards provide access to a fast 4G network. While their coverage might not be as comprehensive as Telkomsel's, it's still reliable in many popular areas.

### Indosat Ooredoo
Indosat Ooredoo offers the "IM3" SIM card, which provides a range of data plans for tourists. Their coverage is suitable for most urban and tourist locations, ensuring a consistent online experience during your stay.

## Communication Apps

### WhatsApp
WhatsApp is widely used in Bali for messaging, voice calls, and even video calls. It's an excellent way to stay in touch with friends, family, and fellow travelers. Many businesses, including tour operators and accommodations, also use WhatsApp for customer service.

### Grab

If you're using ride-sharing services, Grab is a popular app that's available in Bali. It offers the convenience of booking rides and even food delivery in some areas. This app can be particularly helpful when navigating busy tourist spots.

### Google Maps

Google Maps is invaluable for navigating Bali's winding streets and complex road networks. It provides real-time traffic updates and directions to various destinations, making it a must-have tool for exploring the island.

## Cafes and Co-Working Spaces

### Digital Nomad-Friendly Locations

Bali has become a hub for digital nomads, and many cafes and co-working spaces offer high-speed internet for those working remotely. These spaces often provide a comfortable environment to work, network, and stay connected.

## Cultural Considerations

**Data Usage and Etiquette**
While staying connected is essential, remember to respect the local culture and the people around you. Avoid using your phone excessively in sacred or quiet areas, and be mindful of data usage, especially if you're on a prepaid plan.

In the modern era, maintaining a connection to the world while experiencing the beauty of Bali is both possible and convenient. With a variety of internet connectivity options, reliable mobile networks, and essential communication apps, you can seamlessly blend the allure of the island's natural wonders with the practicality of staying informed and connected. By leveraging these tools wisely, you can enhance your Bali adventure and capture every moment of your journey in this enchanting paradise.

# CHAPTER 10: Itineraries for Every Traveler

## 10.1 3 Days in Bali: Family-Focused Itinerary

Bali is a fantastic destination for families, offering a blend of cultural experiences, outdoor adventures, and relaxation. This 3-day itinerary is designed to help you make the most of your family vacation in Bali, ensuring that everyone, from the youngest to the oldest, has a memorable and enjoyable time.*

### Day 1: Exploring Cultural Wonder

Morning:
- Breakfast at the Hotel: Start your day with a hearty breakfast at your hotel, fueling up for the adventures ahead.

- Visit Batuan Village: Immerse your family in Balinese culture with a visit to Batuan Village. Explore the traditional Balinese compound, observe local artisans at work, and witness intricate Batuan-style paintings.

Afternoon:
- Lunch at a Local Warung: Enjoy a flavorful lunch at a local warung, savoring authentic Balinese dishes.

- Monkey Forest: Head to the Ubud Monkey Forest, where kids and adults alike will be enchanted by the playful antics of the resident monkeys. Explore the lush surroundings and ancient temples within the sanctuary.

Evening:
- Traditional Dance Performance: Attend a captivating Balinese dance performance. The colorful costumes and expressive storytelling will captivate the entire family.

- Dinner in Ubud: Dine at a family-friendly restaurant in Ubud, offering a mix of local and international cuisine.

**Day 2: Outdoor Adventures**

Morning:
- Breakfast at the Hotel: Start the day with another delicious breakfast at your hotel.

- Waterbom Bali: Spend the morning at Waterbom Bali, a water park with a variety of slides, pools, and attractions suitable for all ages. Cool off and have a blast in the tropical paradise.

Afternoon:
- Lunch at Waterbom: Enjoy a leisurely lunch within the water park's premises.

- Tanjung Benoa Water Sports: Head to Tanjung Benoa for an afternoon of water sports and beach fun. Try parasailing, banana boat rides, or a thrilling jet ski adventure.

Evening:
- Sunset at Uluwatu Temple: Make your way to Uluwatu Temple for a spectacular sunset view. Witness a traditional Kecak dance performance against the backdrop of the ocean and cliffs.

- Seafood Dinner on Jimbaran Beach: Dine on the sandy shores of Jimbaran Beach, enjoying a seafood feast as the stars twinkle above.

**Day 3: Nature and Relaxation**

Morning:
- Breakfast at the Hotel: Savor your last Balinese breakfast at the hotel.

- Treetop Adventure Park: Spend the morning at the Bali Treetop Adventure Park in Bedugul.

Embark on thrilling ziplines and treetop courses amidst the lush forest.

Afternoon:
- Lunch in Bedugul: Enjoy a picnic lunch amidst the serene surroundings of Bedugul.

- Bali Botanic Garden: Explore the Bali Botanic Garden nearby. Stroll through various themed gardens, learn about local plant species, and take in the beauty of nature.

Evening:
- Relax by the Beach: Return to your hotel and spend the evening by the beach or pool, enjoying quality family time.

- Farewell Dinner: Indulge in a farewell dinner at the hotel's restaurant or venture out to a nearby eatery to create lasting memories over a delightful meal.

This 3-day family-focused itinerary provides a balanced blend of cultural exploration, exciting adventures, and tranquil relaxation. From discovering traditional villages and experiencing local performances to indulging in water park fun and exploring natural wonders, your family will leave Bali with cherished memories of a wonderful vacation together. Remember to adjust the itinerary based on your family's preferences and pace, and make sure to soak in the unique beauty and warmth of Bali throughout your journey.

## 10.2 5 Days in Bali: Romantic Escape

Day 1: Arrival
Arrive in Bali and check into a luxurious beachfront villa. Spend the afternoon relaxing by the pool or taking a stroll on the pristine beach. Enjoy a romantic dinner at a seaside restaurant, savoring Balinese delicacies.

Day 2: Ubud Exploration
Head to Ubud, known for its lush landscapes and artistic vibe. Visit the Sacred Monkey Forest Sanctuary and explore local markets. In the evening, attend a traditional Balinese dance performance and dine at a cozy restaurant nestled in the rice terraces.

Day 3: Waterfalls and Spa
Embark on a waterfall-hopping adventure, visiting Tegenungan and Tirta Empul waterfalls. Enjoy a refreshing dip in the natural pools. Later, indulge in a couples' spa treatment using traditional Balinese techniques.

Day 4: Sunrise Volcano Trek and Hot Springs
Rise early for a sunrise trek up Mount Batur. Witness breathtaking views and enjoy a romantic breakfast at the summit. Afterward, relax in natural hot springs with stunning mountain vistas.

Day 5: Beaches and Sunset Cruise
Spend the morning at one of Bali's beautiful beaches, like Seminyak or Nusa Dua. In the evening, embark on a private sunset cruise, complete with a gourmet dinner and breathtaking views of the coastline.

Please note that activities and places may need to be adjusted based on your preferences.

### *10.3 7 Days in Bali: Adventure and Culture*

Day 1: Arrival in Ubud
Arrive in Ubud, the cultural heart of Bali. Explore the Ubud Monkey Forest, visit art galleries, and stroll through the Ubud Market. Immerse yourself in Balinese culture with traditional dance performances.

Day 2: Rice Terraces and Cycling
Embark on a cycling tour through the stunning Tegallalang Rice Terraces. Experience rural life as

you cycle past lush landscapes and traditional villages. Visit a local family compound to learn about daily life.

Day 3: Mount Batur Sunrise Trek
Start early for a challenging trek up Mount Batur. Witness the sunrise from the summit and enjoy breakfast cooked by volcanic steam. Descend to visit nearby hot springs and relax.

Day 4: Water Adventures
Travel to the east coast for water activities. Try white-water rafting on the Ayung River or explore underwater beauty while snorkeling in Amed. Unwind on Amed's volcanic black sand beaches.

Day 5: North Bali Exploration
Visit the iconic Ulun Danu Beratan Temple located by Lake Beratan. Continue to the Gitgit Waterfall and explore the lesser-known Munduk area, known for its lush landscapes and charming villages.

Day 6: Uluwatu and Sea Temple
Head to Uluwatu to witness the famous Kecak dance performance against a stunning ocean backdrop. Explore Uluwatu Temple and its dramatic clifftop setting. Enjoy a seafood dinner on the beach.

Day 7: Beach Time and Departure
Spend your last day unwinding on Seminyak's beaches. Enjoy surfing or simply relax by the sea. In the evening, catch a beautiful sunset before departing from Bali.

Remember, Bali's offerings are diverse, so feel free to customize this itinerary based on your preferences.

# CHAPTER 11: Additional Resources

## 11.1 Useful Apps and Websites

**1. Transportation Apps:**
- Gojek: Similar to Uber, it offers ride-hailing, food delivery, and even motorcycle taxis (ojeks).

- Grab: Another popular ride-hailing app for cars and motorcycles.

**2. Navigation Apps:**
- Google Maps: Helpful for navigating Bali's intricate roads and finding points of interest.

- Waze: Offers real-time traffic updates, useful for avoiding congested routes.

**3. Language and Communication:**
- Google Translate: Translates languages in real-time, useful for communicating with locals.

- Bali Buddy: Offers useful Balinese phrases and local etiquette tips.

**4. Accommodation Apps:**
- Agoda: Provides a wide range of accommodation options, including hotels, resorts, and villas.

- Airbnb: Great for finding unique local stays, from traditional Balinese homes to luxury villas.

## 5. Food and Dining:
- Zomato: Helps you discover and review local restaurants, cafes, and eateries.

- Bali Foodies: Offers restaurant recommendations and food delivery options.

## 6. Travel Planning and Information:
- TripAdvisor: Read reviews, find attractions, and plan activities based on other travelers' experiences.

- Bali.com: Offers comprehensive travel information, including guides on beaches, activities, and culture.

## 7. Currency Conversion and Finance:
- XE Currency: Helps you calculate exchange rates to make informed financial decisions.

- ATM Locator: Websites like Mastercard's ATM Locator can help you find nearby ATMs with lower withdrawal fees.

## 8. Weather and Safety:

- AccuWeather: Provides detailed weather forecasts to help you plan your activities.

- Smart Traveler Enrollment Program (STEP): If you're a U.S. citizen, enroll in STEP for safety updates from the local embassy.

## 9. Social and Networking:
- Meetup: Find local events and meet fellow travelers or expats.

- Couchsurfing: Connect with locals and travelers for meetups, events, and cultural exchanges.

## 10. Local Culture and Experiences:
- Klook: Offers discounted tickets to attractions, activities, and tours.

- Bali Go Live: Stay updated on local events, workshops, and cultural experiences.

## 11. Health and Medical Assistance:
- InternationalSOS: Provides medical and travel assistance services.

- Halodoc: Allows you to consult with doctors online for minor health concerns.

**12. Connectivity:**
   - Telkomsel SIM Card: Purchase a local SIM card for reliable data connectivity throughout your trip.

**13. Eco-Friendly Travel:**
   - Refill My Bottle: Helps you locate nearby places to refill your reusable water bottle, reducing plastic waste.

Remember, it's a good practice to download these apps and familiarize yourself with them before your trip. Internet connectivity might vary in certain areas, so having essential apps downloaded offline can be helpful. Also, make sure to check reviews and ratings before relying heavily on any particular app or website.

### *11.2 Emergency Contacts*

Absolutely, having access to emergency contacts while traveling in Bali is crucial for your safety and well-being. Here's an extensive list of emergency contacts and resources you should keep in mind:

**1. General Emergency Services:**
   - Police: 110
   - Ambulance: 118
   - Fire Department: 113

**2. Medical Emergencies:**
- BIMC Hospital Bali: A well-regarded private hospital with multiple locations across the island.
- Emergency Contact: +62 361 761 263
- Siloam Hospitals: Another reputable private hospital chain in Bali.
- Emergency Contact: +62 361 779 900
- International SOS Bali Clinic: Provides medical assistance and advice to travelers.
- Emergency Contact: +62 811 380 8242

**3. Tourist Police:**
- Tourist Police Office: Specialized in assisting tourists with legal matters and emergencies.
- Emergency Contact: +62 361 754 599

**4. Consulates and Embassies:**
- Consulate General of the United States - Bali:
- Emergency Contact: +62 361 233 605
- Australian Consulate - Bali:
- Emergency Contact: +62 361 241 118
- British Consulate - Bali:
- Emergency Contact: +62 361 270 601
- Canadian Consulate - Bali:
- Emergency Contact: +62 361 202 1302

**5. Roadside Assistance:**

- Bali Police Traffic Unit: For accidents and traffic-related emergencies.
 - Emergency Contact: 110 or +62 361 759 687

**6. Natural Disaster Information:**
 - Bali's Disaster Management Agency (BPBD):
 - Website: bali.bnpb.go.id

**7. Search and Rescue:**
 - Basarnas Bali (National Search and Rescue Agency):
 - Emergency Contact: +62 361 751 111

**8. Animal Emergencies:**
 - Bali Animal Welfare Association (BAWA): For injured or mistreated animals.
 - Emergency Contact: +62 811 389 004

**9. Transportation Safety:**
 - Airport Information: Ngurah Rai International Airport (Denpasar)
 - Contact: +62 361 935 1011

**10. Local Contacts:**
 - Hotel Reception: They can assist you with emergencies and provide local guidance.
 - Local Tour Operators: If you're on a guided tour, their contacts can be helpful in emergencies.

- Local Friends or Acquaintances: Having local contacts can offer valuable assistance.

**11. Communication Tips:**
- Learn Basic Local Phrases: Knowing a few local phrases can help you communicate during emergencies.
- Keep Your Phone Charged: Ensure you have a working phone and charger at all times.
- Carry Important Documents: Keep copies of your passport, travel insurance, and emergency contacts.

Remember, in the case of an emergency, try to remain calm and seek assistance immediately. It's also a good idea to keep a list of these emergency contacts in both digital and print formats for easy access. Prioritize your safety and well-being at all times while traveling in Bali.

Printed in Great Britain
by Amazon